Welcome to BPP Learning Media's ICAEW **Passcards** for **Tax Compliance.**

- They **save you time**. Important topics are summarised for you.

- They incorporate **diagrams** to kick start your memory.

- They follow the overall **structure** of the ICAEW Study Manuals, but BPP Learning Media's ICAEW **Passcards** are not just a condensed book. Each card has been separately designed for clear presentation. Topics are self contained and can be grasped visually.

- ICAEW **Passcards** are **just the right size** for pockets, briefcases and bags.

- ICAEW **Passcards focus on the exams** you will be facing.

Run through the complete set of **Passcards** as often as you can during your final revision period. The day before the exam, go through the **Passcards** again! You will then be well on your way to passing your exams.

Good luck!

Contents

For exams in 2014

ICAEW Tax Compliance
FA2013

Second edition 2013

ISBN 9781 4727 0391 0

British Library Cataloguing-in-Publication Data

A catalogue record for this publication is available from the British Library

Published by

BPP Learning Media Ltd,
BPP House, Aldine Place,
142-144 Uxbridge Road,
London W12 8AA

www.bpp.com/learningmedia

Printed in the United Kingdom by Ricoh

Ricoh House
Ullswater Crescent
Coulsdon
CR5 2HR

The contents of this book are intended as a guide and not professional advice. Although every effort has been made to ensure that the contents of this book are correct at the time of going to press, BPP Learning Media makes no warranty that the information in this publication is accurate or complete and accept no liability for any loss or damage suffered by any person acting or refraining from acting as a result of the material in this publication.

Every effort has been made to contact the copyright holders of any material reproduced within this publication. If any have been inadvertently overlooked, BPP Learning Media will be pleased to make the appropriate credits in any subsequent reprints or editions.

1: Income tax computation

Topic List

Charge to income tax

Gifts to charity

Interest payments

Jointly owned assets

Allowances for taxpayers born before 6.4.48

The calculation of income tax is key in the Tax Compliance exam.

This chapter first helps you to identify chargeable and exempt income, drawing the taxable items together in the income tax computation.

It also explains how to deal with gifts to charity and how higher tax allowances are available for older taxpayers.

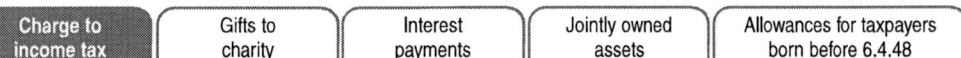

Types of income

The main types of income for individuals are:

- Income from employment
- Profits of trades
- Property income

    Non-savings

- **Savings** income (eg interest)
- **Dividends**
- Other miscellaneous income

Exempt income

- Interest on NS&I certificates
- Income arising on ISAs
- Betting and lottery winnings
- Premium Bond winnings
- Social security benefits
- First £4,250 of rent under rent a room scheme
- Scholarships
- Income tax repayment interest
- Universal credit

Leave exempt income out of personal tax computations but state exempt

Income taxed at source

Many types of investment income are taxed at source: for every £100 of income, the individual only receives £80 of interest or £90 of dividends from UK companies. The taxable income in both cases is £100, but credit is given for the tax suffered.

This applies to bank and building society interest

Tax credits on dividends can be offset to reduce a tax bill but are never repaid to a taxpayer. Tax credits on other taxed income can be repaid. Offset the tax credits on dividends first against income tax liability.

Income received gross

- Property income
- Trading income
- Miscellaneous income
- Interest from NS&I (i) Direct Saver and (ii) Investment Accounts
- Treasury stock interest
- Interest received by non-tax payer who has self certified
- Interest on loans between individuals

Usually child or pensioner

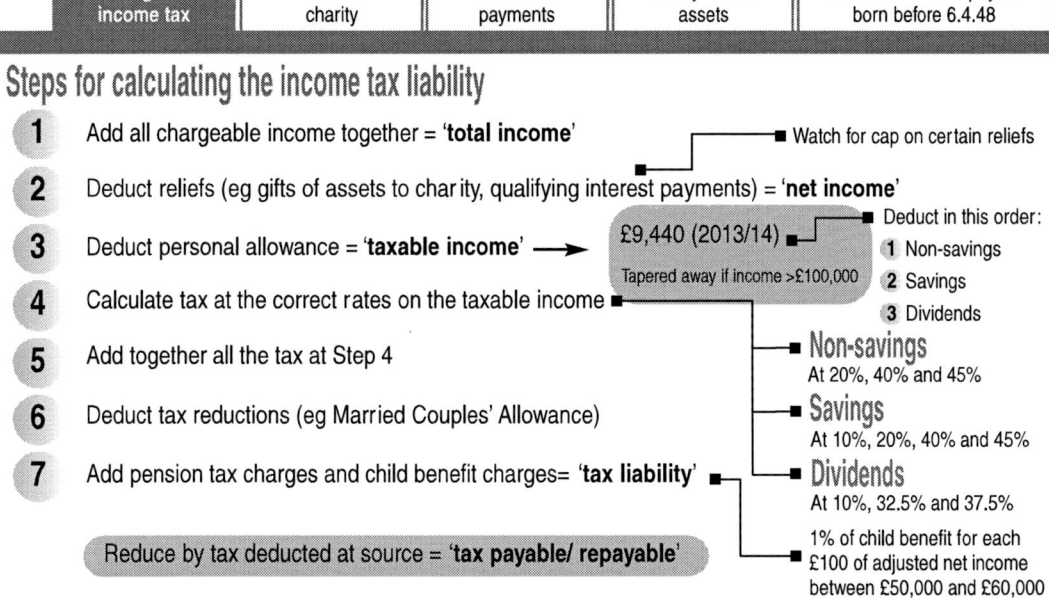

| Charge to income tax | Gifts to charity | Interest payments | Jointly owned assets | Allowances for taxpayers born before 6.4.48 |

Steps for calculating the income tax liability

1 Add all chargeable income together = '**total income**'

■ Watch for cap on certain reliefs

2 Deduct reliefs (eg gifts of assets to charity, qualifying interest payments) = '**net income**'

3 Deduct personal allowance = '**taxable income**' → £9,440 (2013/14)

Tapered away if income >£100,000

■ Deduct in this order:
1 Non-savings
2 Savings
3 Dividends

4 Calculate tax at the correct rates on the taxable income ■

5 Add together all the tax at Step 4

6 Deduct tax reductions (eg Married Couples' Allowance)

7 Add pension tax charges and child benefit charges = '**tax liability**' ■

Reduce by tax deducted at source = '**tax payable/ repayable**'

■ **Non-savings**
At 20%, 40% and 45%

■ **Savings**
At 10%, 20%, 40% and 45%

■ **Dividends**
At 10%, 32.5% and 37.5%

1% of child benefit for each £100 of adjusted net income between £50,000 and £60,000

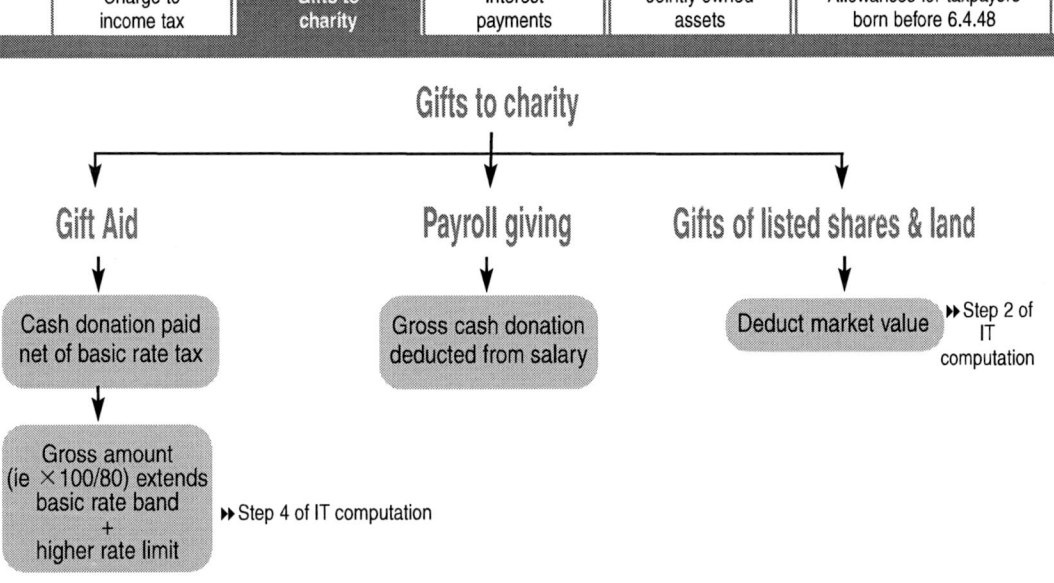

Gifts to charity

Gift Aid

Cash donation paid net of basic rate tax

↓

Gross amount (ie × 100/80) extends basic rate band + higher rate limit

▸▸ Step 4 of IT computation

Payroll giving

Gross cash donation deducted from salary

Gifts of listed shares & land

Deduct market value

▸▸ Step 2 of IT computation

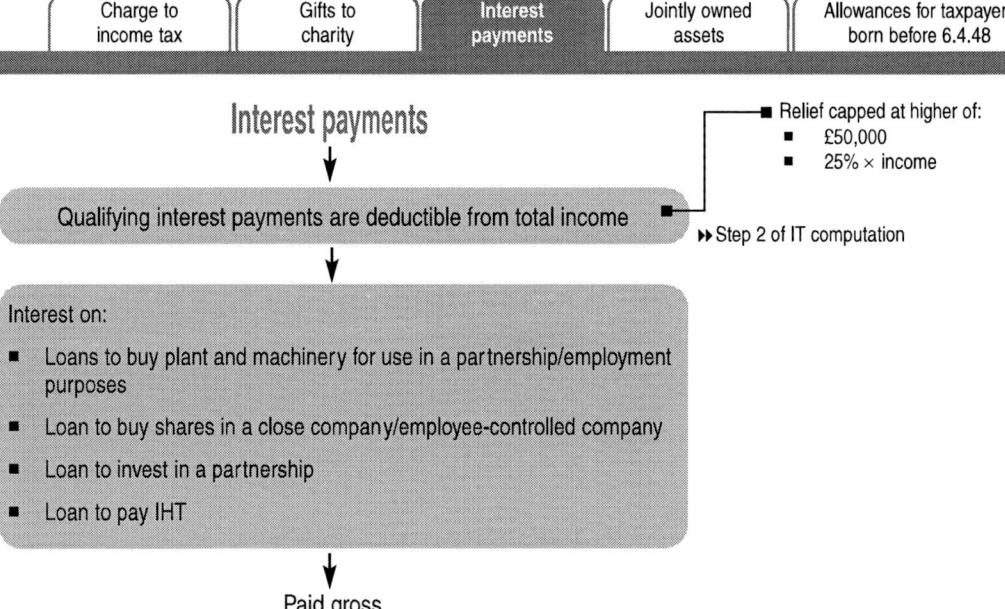

Interest payments

↓

Qualifying interest payments are deductible from total income

■ Relief capped at higher of:
  ■ £50,000
  ■ 25% × income

▸▸ Step 2 of IT computation

↓

Interest on:

■ Loans to buy plant and machinery for use in a partnership/employment purposes

■ Loan to buy shares in a close company/employee-controlled company

■ Loan to invest in a partnership

■ Loan to pay IHT

↓

Paid gross

Jointly owned assets

1 Spouses share income equally unless dividends from shares in family company

2 Can make declaration to be taxed on income to which actually entitled

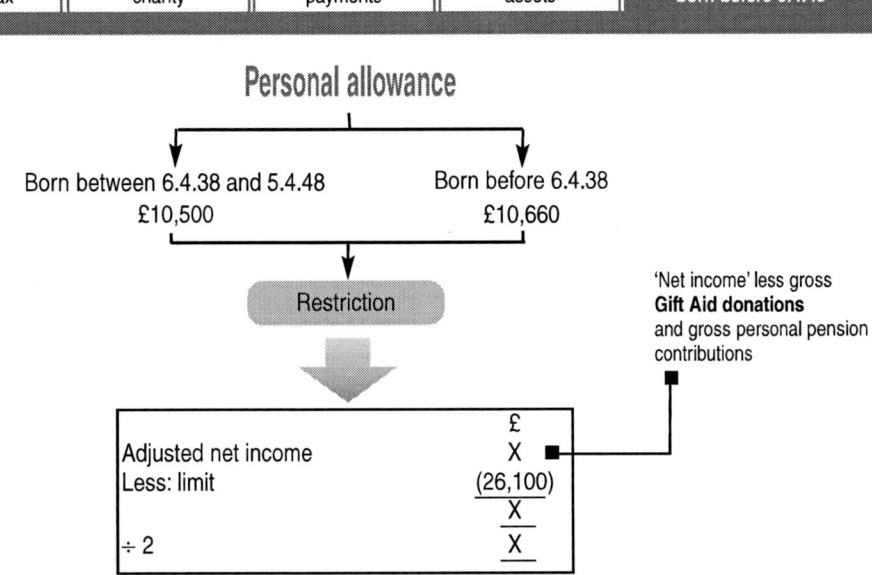

Personal allowance

Born between 6.4.38 and 5.4.48
£10,500

Born before 6.4.38
£10,660

Restriction

'Net income' less gross **Gift Aid donations** and gross personal pension contributions

	£
Adjusted net income	X
Less: limit	(26,100)
	X
÷ 2	X

Married couple's allowance

Allowance for older married couples and civil partners which reduces the income tax liability (rather than the income itself) as a **tax reduction** ◄◄ Step 6

Based on:
- Age of elder spouse
- Husband's income if married before 5.12.05
- Higher earner if married on/after 5.12.05

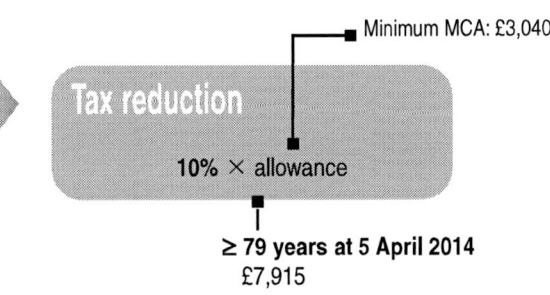

Minimum MCA: £3,040

Tax reduction

10% × allowance

≥ **79 years at 5 April 2014**
£7,915

Watch for restriction where adjusted net income > £26,100

Notes

2: Property income

Topic List

This chapter will help you to understand the tax treatment of property income.

It also covers how to identify and deal with furnished holiday accommodation as well as how to tax certain lease premiums.

Property income

Broadly rent from UK property.

Computation

Exception
Keep a separate pool of profits/losses from letting furnished holiday accommodation

▸▸ see later

1 Calculate property income on an accruals basis for the tax year (ie 6 April to 5 April)

2 Rents and **expenses** of all properties are pooled to give a single property income figure

3 Net **losses** are carried forward against future income from the UK property business

Expenses

- Legal and professional costs
- Mortgage and other interest
- Ancillary services eg gardening
- Insurance
- Furnishings
- Repairs and maintenance
- Landlord energy savings allowance

- For furnished lettings, a 10% wear and tear allowance can be claimed instead of capital allowances

Rent a room relief

Rent of up to £4,250 a year on rooms in the landlord's main residence is exempt

Real Estate Investment Trusts (REIT)

> Company that is exempt from corporation tax on some of its income

⬇

Distributions to investors

Paid from tax-exempt income ← → Paid from non tax-exempt income

⬇ ⬇

Come with 20% tax credit | Come with 10% tax credit

⬇ ⬇

Gross up at 100/80 | Gross up at 100/90

Property Authorised Investment Funds (AIF)

> Fund with investments in property or shares

⬇

Distributions to investors

Property or interest ← → Dividend

⬇ ⬇

Come with 20% tax credit | Come with 10% tax credit

⬇ ⬇

Gross up at 100/80 | Gross up at 100/90

2: Property income

Qualifying property

Must be:

- In the UK or elsewhere in EEA
- Furnished
- Let on a commercial basis
- Available for letting for 210 days in the tax year
- Actually let for 105 days in the tax year
- Not in **longer term occupation** for more than 155 days during the tax year

- Continuous periods of more than 31 days during which the accommodation is in the same occupation

Losses on FHL can only be set against income from the same FHL business

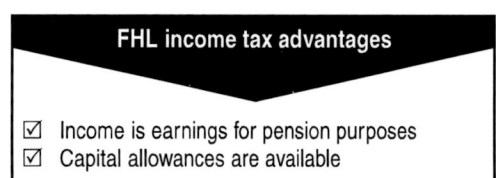

FHL income tax advantages

☑ Income is earnings for pension purposes
☑ Capital allowances are available

Lease premiums

If a lease is granted for 50 years or less for a premium (**P**), the part of the premium taxable as rent on the landlord is:

$$P \times \frac{50 - Y}{50}$$ ■———■ **Y** = number of years on the lease *minus* 1

If tenant is a trader can divide this amount over length of lease and deduct from trading profits

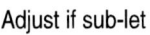

Adjust if sub-let

Notes

3: Pensions

A single regime applies to all pensions, whether occupational (ie run by an employer) or personal.

Pension contributions are a tax efficient way of saving for retirement.

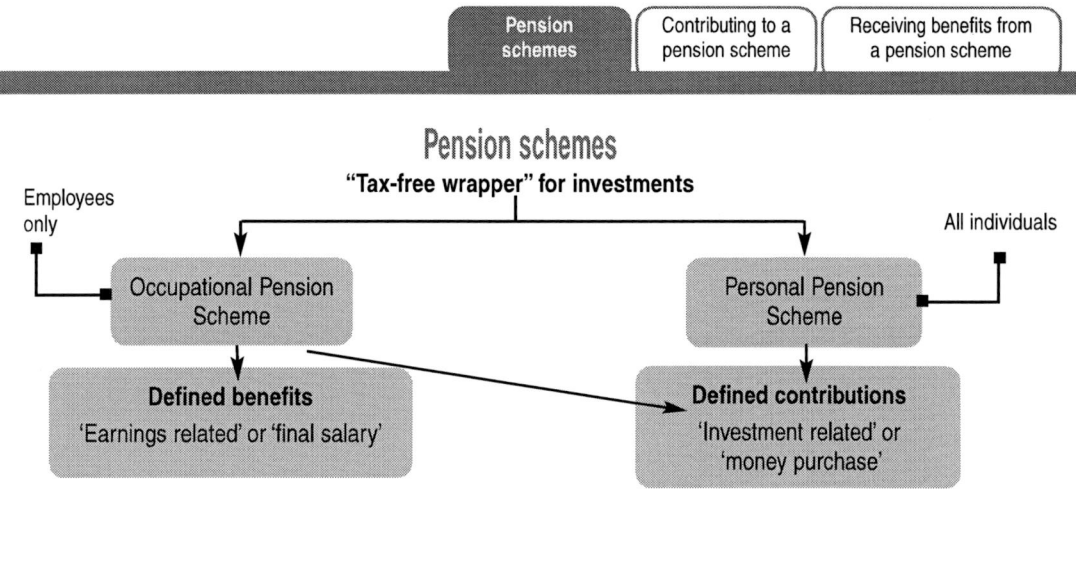

Annual limit

Maximum contribution Is higher of

- Relevant earnings
- £3,600

■ Employment income, trading income and furnished holiday accommodation income

Tax relief

1 *Personal pension*

- Paid net so automatic 20% tax relief
- Higher rate taxpayers extend basic rate band by gross contributions (ie × 100/80 – same method as for Gift Aid)
- Additional rate tax payers extend basic rate band and higher rate limit by gross contribution
  ▸▸ Step 4 of IT computation

Annual allowance

£50,000 (2013/14)

Annual allowance tax charge on contributions in excess of the annual allowance at individual's marginal rate

2 *Occupational pension*

Deduct gross employee contributions directly from earnings to find net earnings ('net pay arrangements')

3: Pensions

Carry forward of unused annual allowance

Unused annual allowance (AA) can be carried forward for three years

- For 2010/11 (earliest year for carry forward in 2013/14) compare pension contributions to an assumed AA of £50,000 (as AA only introduced from 6 April 2011)
- Use unused annual allowance on FIFO basis

Employer contributions

- Tax free benefit for employee
- Count towards allowances (annual & lifetime) ▸▸ see later
- Usually deductible from trade income for employer

Employers can contribute to either type of pension

Lifetime allowance

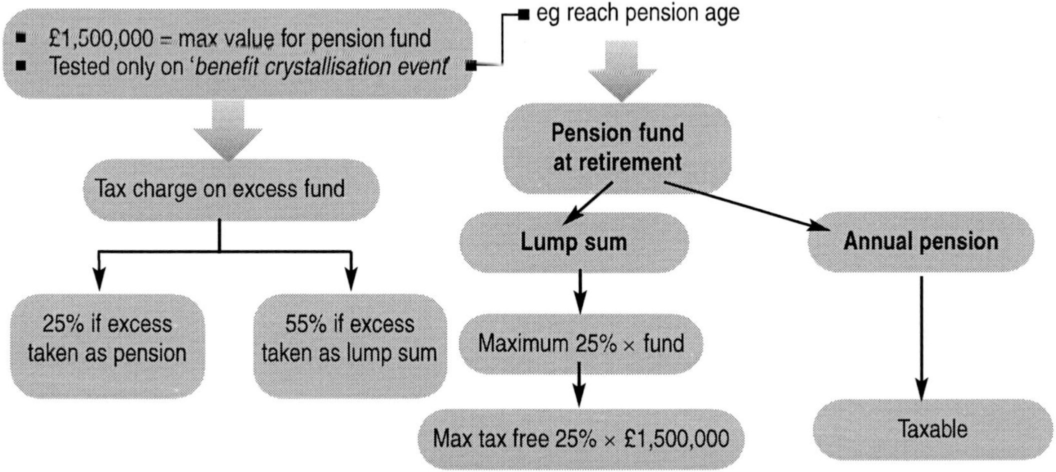

- £1,500,000 = max value for pension fund
- Tested only on '*benefit crystallisation event*'

■ eg reach pension age

Pension fund at retirement

Tax charge on excess fund

- 25% if excess taken as pension
- 55% if excess taken as lump sum

Lump sum

Annual pension

Maximum 25% × fund

Max tax free 25% × £1,500,000

Taxable

Notes

4: Employment income

Topic List

Charge to tax on employment income

Allowable deductions

Statutory mileage rate scheme

Taxable and exempt benefits

In this chapter, we review the receipts basis and the main taxable and exempt benefits and then extend your knowledge to include the special receipts rules for directors, further rules on car and fuel benefits, employment related loans, private use of assets and transfers of assets.

We also cover allowable deductions from employment income and the statutory mileage rate scheme.

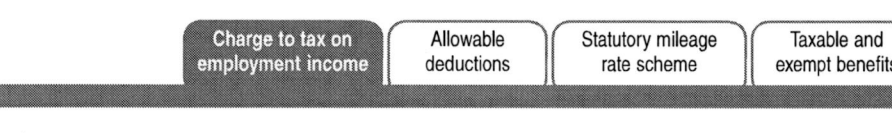

Employment income

Employees/directors are taxed on income from their employment:

- General earnings ■━━━━━━━━ ■ eg salary, benefits
- Specific employment income

Earnings are taxed in the year in which they are received.

The general rule for date of receipt is the earlier of:

- The time payment is made
- The time entitlement to payment arises

Directors are deemed to receive earnings on the earliest of the following:

- The time given by the general rule
- The time the amount is credited in the company's accounting records
- The end of the company's period of account (if the amount has been determined by then)
- When the amount is determined, if this after the end of the company's period of account

General rule

Expenses must be included as earnings and can only be deducted if they are incurred *wholly, exclusively and necessarily* in performing the duties of employment.

Expenses specifically deductible against earnings:

1. **Qualifying travel expenses** – costs the employee incurs travelling in the performance of his duties and/or travelling to or from a place attended in the performance of duties

   - Normal commuting does not qualify
   - Relief is available for expenses incurred by a site based employee or an employee working at a temporary location on a secondment of 24 months or less

2. Most **entertaining expenses** unless part of round sum allowance

3. **Subscriptions** to HMRC approved professional bodies

   No need to report expense on tax return if employer has agreed an HMRC dispensation

Round sum allowance

- Deduction only available if wholly and exclusively incurred for the purpose of *employer's trade,* ie NOT client entertaining
- Employer can deduct the *full* allowance

Mileage allowance

Tax free for all employees up to:
45p	≤ 10,000 business miles
25p	> 10,000 business miles

- Payments over these amounts - excess is TAXABLE
- Payments below these amounts - underpayment is DEDUCTIBLE

Non cash benefits

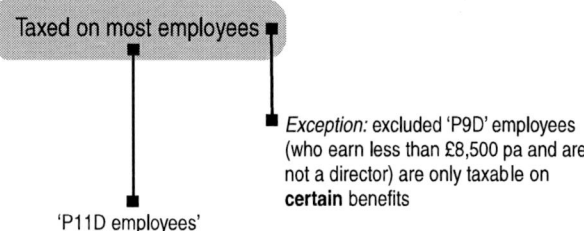

Taxed on most employees

'P11D employees'

Exception: excluded 'P9D' employees (who earn less than £8,500 pa and are not a director) are only taxable on **certain** benefits

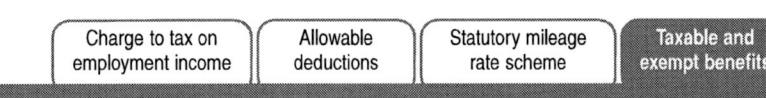

The following benefits are taxable on P9D and P11D employees.

General rule

Use if no specific rule

- **Excluded employees:** 2nd hand value
- **P11D employees:** cost to the employer

Vouchers

Cost of providing
- Cash/non-cash vouchers
- Credit token (eg credit cards)

Accommodation

Annual value of accommodation is a taxable benefit on all employees, unless job related.

Additional charge if costs more than £75,000

excess × official rate of interest at the start of the tax year

The following benefits are only taxable on P11D employees.

Living expenses

Living expenses connected with accommodation (eg gas bills) are taxable.

- If job related accommodation, the maximum amount taxable is 10% × net earnings.
- Furniture available for private use is taxable @ 20% × market value when first provided.

Cars

- The annual taxable benefit for the private use of a car is (list price of car – capital contributions) × %

Max £5,000

- Reduced by employee contributions
- Time apportioned if available for private use for part of year

- % depends on CO_2 emissions
- Zero emissions = 0%
- Up to 75g/km: % = **5%**
- Up to 94g/km: % = **10%**
- Emissions of 95g/km: = **11%**
- % increases by 1% for each 5g/km up to a **maximum of 35%**
- Additional **3%** for diesel cars (max still 35%)

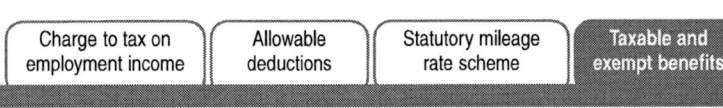

Car fuel

- Fuel for private use is charged as % of base figure (£21,100 in 2013/14)

- Same % as car benefit

- No reduction for partial reimbursement by employee

Vans

- £3,000 for unrestricted private use

- £564 fuel benefit

Loans ■————■ Use average or strict method

Private use of asset ■—■ No benefit on provision of computer if private use insignificant

1. Loans of over £5,000 give rise to taxable benefits equal to the difference between the actual interest and interest at the official rate.

2. A write-off of a loan gives rise to a taxable benefit equal to the amount written off.

■ If an asset is made available for private use, the annual taxable benefit is:

   20% × MV when asset first provided

■ Deduct any employee contributions.

If significant private use of computer calculate benefit using the 20% rule and then reduce for business use

Use market value rule only if asset is: ■
- Car
- Van
- Bicycle

Asset transferred

If an asset is given to the employee the taxable benefit is the higher of:

(i) Original cost *less* amounts already taxed
(ii) Market value at date of gift
less price paid by employee.

4: Employment income

Exempt benefits

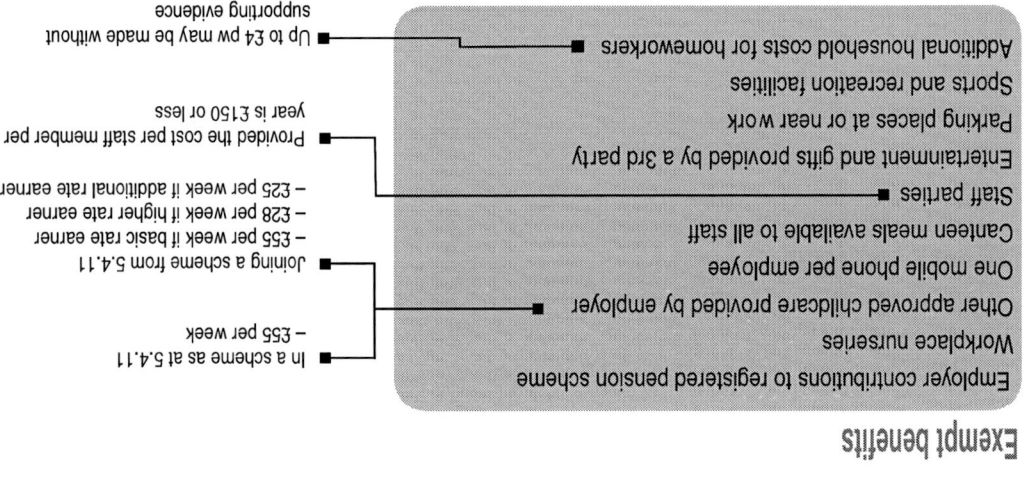

Employer contributions to registered pension scheme

Workplace nurseries — ■ In a scheme as at 5.4.11
 – £55 per week

Other approved childcare provided by employer — ■ Joining a scheme from 5.4.11
 – £55 per week if basic rate earner
 – £28 per week if higher rate earner
 – £25 per week if additional rate earner

One mobile phone per employee

Canteen meals available to all staff

Staff parties — ■ Provided the cost per staff member per year is £150 or less

Entertainment and gifts provided by a 3rd party

Parking places at or near work

Sports and recreation facilities

Additional household costs for homeworkers — ■ Up to £4 pw may be made without supporting evidence

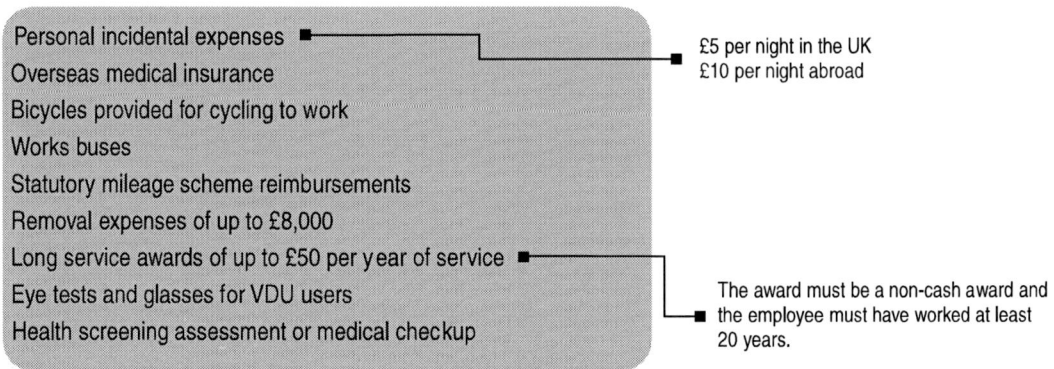

Personal incidental expenses — £5 per night in the UK / £10 per night abroad

Overseas medical insurance

Bicycles provided for cycling to work

Works buses

Statutory mileage scheme reimbursements

Removal expenses of up to £8,000

Long service awards of up to £50 per year of service — The award must be a non-cash award and the employee must have worked at least 20 years.

Eye tests and glasses for VDU users

Health screening assessment or medical checkup

Notes

5: Trading income

Topic List

Badges of trade

Adjustment of profits

Basis periods

Change of accounting date

Patent royalties

You have already met the basics of trading income in the Principles of Taxation exam.

This chapter reviews the basic topics of the badges of trade, adjustment to profits, allowable/disallowable expenditure and basis periods. It then extends your knowledge to enable you to make a full adjustment of profit calculation for a sole trader.

It also covers the change of accounting date rules and treatment of patent royalties.

Badges of trade

- Profit seeking motive
- Number of transactions
- Nature of the asset
- Existence of similar trading transactions
- Changes to the asset
- Way the sale was carried out
- Source of finance
- Interval of time between purchase and sale
- Method of acquisition

If, on applying the badges of trade, HMRC concludes that a trade is being carried on, the profits are taxable as trading income.

Adjustment of profits

> To arrive at taxable trading profits, the net accounts profit must be adjusted.

- Certain items of expenditure are not deductible (ie not allowable) for trading income purposes and must be added back to the net accounts profit when computing trading profits.
- Conversely other items are deductible (ie **allowable**).

Allowable expenditure

> Expenditure incurred **wholly** and **exclusively** for trade purposes

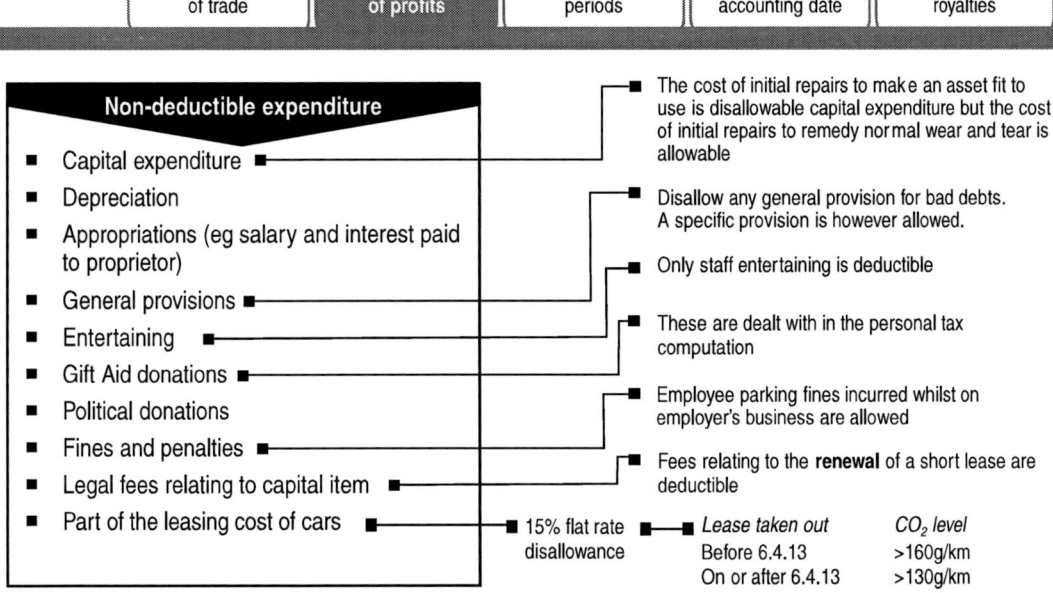

Non-deductible expenditure

- Capital expenditure ■ — The cost of initial repairs to make an asset fit to use is disallowable capital expenditure but the cost of initial repairs to remedy normal wear and tear is allowable
- Depreciation
- Appropriations (eg salary and interest paid to proprietor)
- General provisions ■ — Disallow any general provision for bad debts. A specific provision is however allowed.
- Entertaining ■ — Only staff entertaining is deductible
- Gift Aid donations ■ — These are dealt with in the personal tax computation
- Political donations
- Fines and penalties ■ — Employee parking fines incurred whilst on employer's business are allowed
- Legal fees relating to capital item ■ — Fees relating to the **renewal** of a short lease are deductible
- Part of the leasing cost of cars ■ — 15% flat rate disallowance

Lease taken out	CO₂ level
Before 6.4.13	>160g/km
On or after 6.4.13	>130g/km

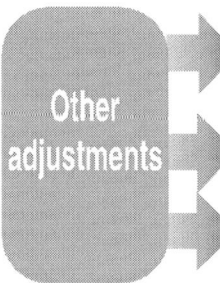

Trading profits not shown in ■────■ eg business owner takes goods for own use without
the accounts must be **added** reimbursing full market value

**Other
adjustments**

Non-trading income in the ■────■ eg rental income, profits on the disposal of fixed assets
accounts must be **deducted** and investment income

Expenditure not shown in the ■────■ eg business expenditure paid personally by the owner
accounts must be **deducted**

Fixed rate expenses

Pre-trading expenditure

Deductible on first day of trading providing:

- Incurred in the 7 years prior to commencement of trade
- Would have been deductible trading expenditure if incurred after trade commenced

Certain small businesses can, instead of actual expenses, deduct fixed rate amounts for:

- Motor vehicles
- Use of home for business purposes
- Business premises partly used as home

Current year basis (CYB)

The basis period for a tax year is normally the period of account ending in the year.

There are special rules which apply in the opening and closing years of a business.

Opening years

Tax year	Basis period
1	*Actual basis*: Date of commencement to following 5 April
2	Depends on length of accounting period ending in year 2:
	(a) 12 months: tax that 12 months
	(b) <12 months: tax the 1st 12 months of trade
	(c) >12 months: tax the 12 months up to the accounting date
	(d) No accounting date ends in year: 6 April - 5 April ('actual' basis)
3	12 months to accounting date in year

Any profits taxed twice as a result of these rules = 'overlap profits'.

Relieved when:
- Business ends
- Change of accounting date

►► see later

Closing year ━━━━ Tax year that trade ends

- Basis period for the final year starts at the end of the basis period for the previous year and ends at cessation.
- Any overlap profits not already relieved are deducted from the final year's profits.

- If business ends in 1st tax year, tax all the profits
- If business ends in 2nd tax year, tax from 6 April until business ends

Change of accounting date

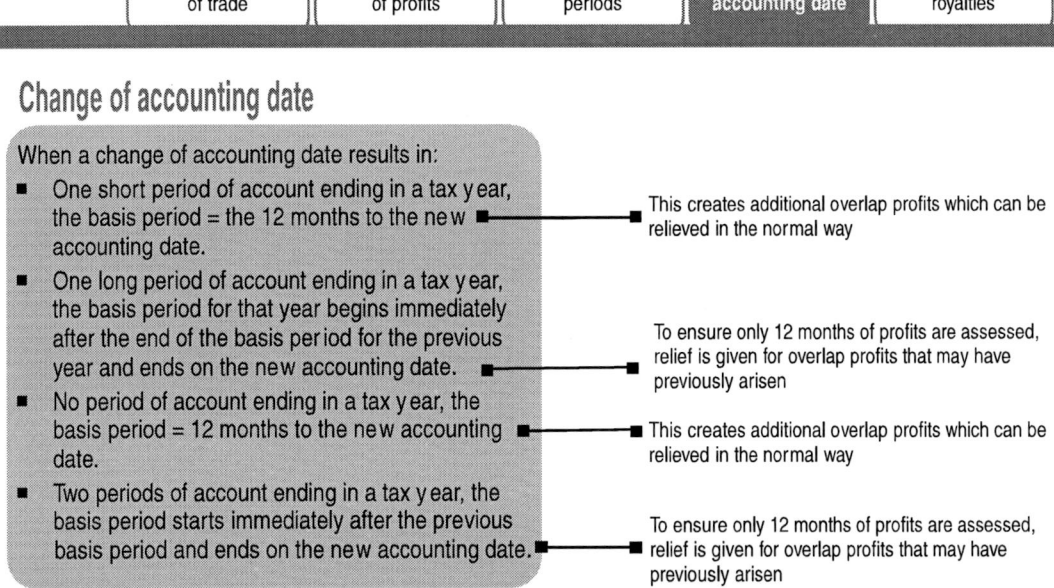

When a change of accounting date results in:

- One short period of account ending in a tax year, the basis period = the 12 months to the new accounting date.

  This creates additional overlap profits which can be relieved in the normal way

- One long period of account ending in a tax year, the basis period for that year begins immediately after the end of the basis period for the previous year and ends on the new accounting date.

  To ensure only 12 months of profits are assessed, relief is given for overlap profits that may have previously arisen

- No period of account ending in a tax year, the basis period = 12 months to the new accounting date.

  This creates additional overlap profits which can be relieved in the normal way

- Two periods of account ending in a tax year, the basis period starts immediately after the previous basis period and ends on the new accounting date.

  To ensure only 12 months of profits are assessed, relief is given for overlap profits that may have previously arisen

Patent royalties

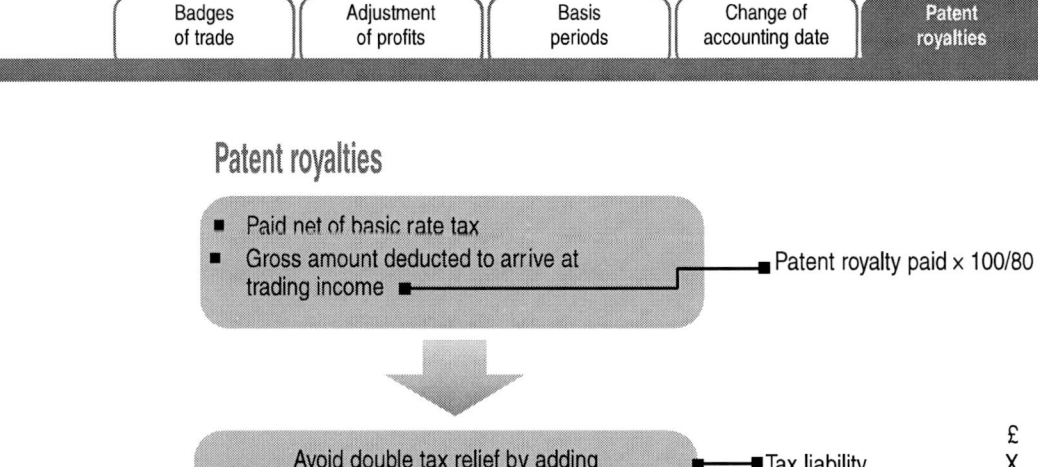

- Paid net of basic rate tax
- Gross amount deducted to arrive at trading income ■————————■ Patent royalty paid × 100/80

Avoid double tax relief by adding tax retained to the tax liability

	£
Tax liability	X
Add: tax on PR paid	X
Tax payable	X

Notes

6: Capital allowances

This chapter reviews the basics of capital allowances on plant and machinery. It then extends your knowledge of this topic by covering aspects such as short and long life assets, hire purchase, business cessations and interaction with VAT.

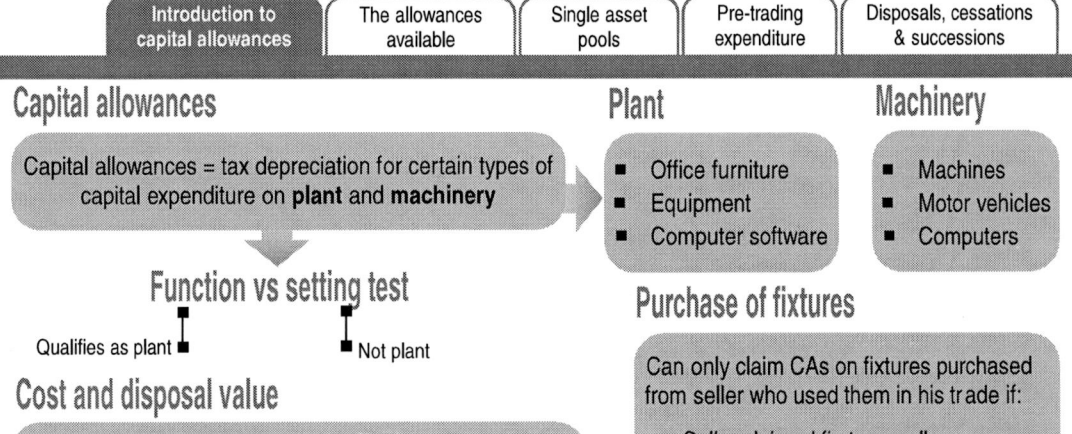

Capital allowances

Capital allowances = tax depreciation for certain types of capital expenditure on **plant** and **machinery**

Function vs setting test

Qualifies as plant ■   ■ Not plant

Cost and disposal value

- If business is VAT registered:
  - If input VAT recoverable: use VAT-exclusive cost
  - If input VAT irrecoverable: use VAT-inclusive cost
- Asset bought on hire purchase (HP) treated as bought for cash at the date of the HP agreement

Plant

- Office furniture
- Equipment
- Computer software

Machinery

- Machines
- Motor vehicles
- Computers

Purchase of fixtures

Can only claim CAs on fixtures purchased from seller who used them in his trade if:

- Seller claimed first year allowances (FYAs)   ▶ see later
- Value of fixtures has been fixed (usually by by joint election)

Main pool

The main pool contains:

- All machinery, fixtures, fittings, equipment
- Vans, forklift trucks, lorries, motorcycles
- Cars:
  - Costing £12,000 or less (pre 6.4.09)
  - CO_2 emissions $\leq$ 160 g/km (6.4.09 – 5.4.13)
  - CO_2 emissions $\leq$ 130 g/km (from 6.4.13)

Writing down allowances (WDAs)

Balance = **tax written down value (TWDV)** ■──

- 18% per annum on a reducing balance basis
- 18% × months/12 in a period that is not 12 months long
- Can claim less CAs than maximum possible

6: Capital allowances

First year allowances (FYAs)

- Replace WDAs in period of expenditure
- **Not pro-rated in short/long accounting periods**
- Not usually available on cars

100% FYA available for:

- Expenditure on certain energy saving equipment
- Technologically-efficient hand dryers
- Low emission cars
- **New** zero emission goods vehicles
- Qualifying R+D capital expenditure
- Expenditure by **companies** in a designated enterprise zone

- From 6.4.13: CO_2 emissions $\leq$95g/km
- Before 6.4.13: CO_2 emissions $\leq$110g/km

Annual Investment Allowance (AIA)

- For all businesses for expenditure up to:
    - £250,000 pa from 1.1.13
    - £25,000 pa between 6.4.12 and 31.12.12
- Scaled up/down for long/short accounting periods
- Allocate AIA to assets eligible for **lowest** rate of WDA
- Balance of expenditure after AIA receives WDA

Special rate pool

Expenditure on:

- Long life assets (LLAs)
- Integral features
  - Thermal insulation and solar panels
  - Cars with CO_2 emissions:
    - >130g/km from 6.4.13
    - >160g/km before 6.4.13

- Electrical systems
- Cold water systems
- Ventilation systems
- Lifts
- Escalators
- Solar shading

- Expected economic working life 25+ years
- Expenditure <£100,000 in period (pro rate for periods <12m)

- WDA = 8% per annum on reducing balance basis
- Given after AIA if available
- Pro rate for a period that is not 12 months long

WDA for small pools

- If balance on main/special rate pool < small pool limit at end of chargeable period, can claim WDA up to small pool limit
- Small pool limit = £1,000 for 12 month chargeable period
- Pro rate for short/long periods

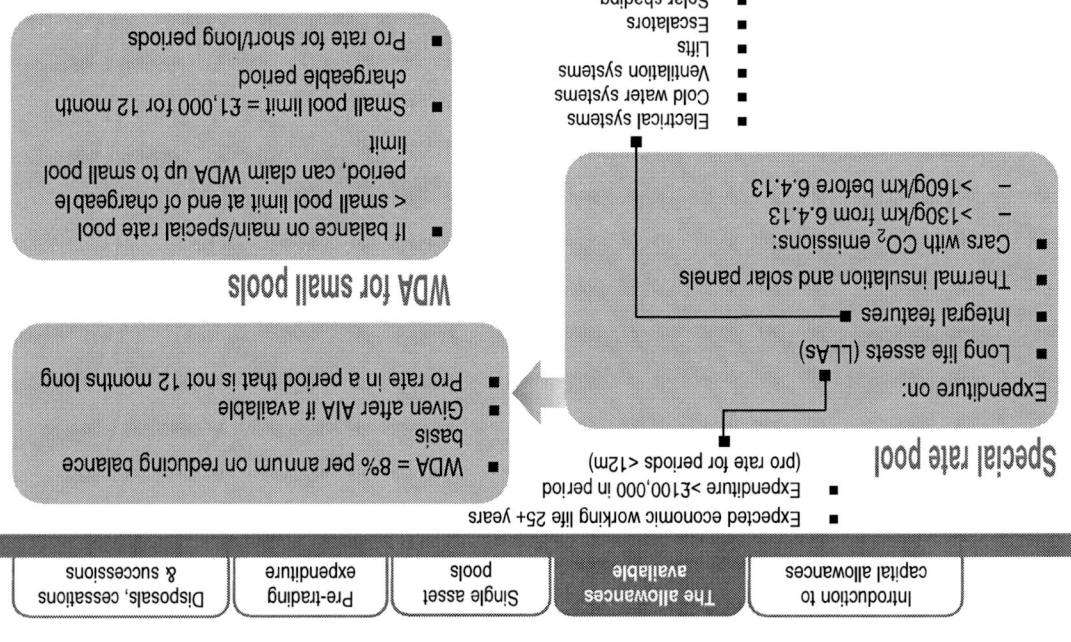

Cars costing > £12,000 (purchased pre 6.4.09)

- Each car has own 'pool'
- WDA at 18% but restricted to £3,000 per annum
- No AIA
- No FYA (unless low emission)

Continue to apply these rules if TWDV b/f on such a car

Otherwise TWDV must be transferred to main pool

Not cars / assets with private use

Short life assets (SLA)

- An **election** can be made to **depool main pool assets**
- Depooled assets must be disposed of within **8 years** of end of the period of acquisition*
- From a planning point of view depooling is useful if balancing allowances are expected

Private use assets

Assets used privately by the owner NOT an employee

- Keep each asset used privately by the business owner in a separate 'pool'
- AIA, FYA and WDA are calculated in full and deducted to calculate TWDV
- BUT can only claim the **business** proportion of allowances

Pre-trading expenditure

- Eligible for capital allowances
- Treated as incurred on first day of trading

6: Capital allowances

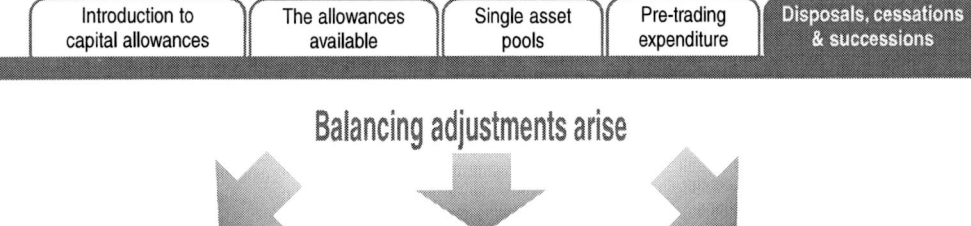

Balancing adjustments arise

- On cessation to deal with balances remaining after deduction of disposal proceeds
  - No WDAs/FYAs/AIAs on cessation

- When a non-pooled asset is sold
  - Pre 6.4.09 cars costing over £12,000/short life assets/ assets with private use

- When a column balance becomes negative
  - This will be a balancing charge (increases profits)

Balancing allowances

- Only arise in the main and special rate pools
- When trade ends – unless qualifies as a small pool

Successions

- When a business is transferred between connected persons, can make election to transfer assets at their TWDVs
- Avoids any balancing adjustments

7: Partnerships

This chapter reviews the basic division of profits between partners and then looks at changes in partnership composition and limited liability partnerships.

Compute trading results for a partnership as a whole in the same way as you would compute the profits for a sole trader (adjusted profit less capital allowances on partnership assets)

Add back partners' salaries and interest as they are 'drawings'

then

Divide results for each period of account between partners

Remember to pro-rate the annual salary/rate of interest if the period is not 12 months long

If the PSA changes during the period of account remember to split the period of account and allocate the profits according to the PSA in each relevant period

First allocate salaries and interest on capital to the partners, then share the firm's results among the partners according to the profit-sharing arrangement (PSA) for the period of account

When a partner joins, the first period of account for his own business runs from the date of joining to the firm's next accounting date. The normal basis period opening years rules apply to him

Each partner is taxed as if he were running his own business, and making profits and losses equal to his share of the firm's results for each period of account

When a partner leaves, the closing year rules apply to him

Limited liability partnerships

Partners' liability is limited to the amount of capital
that they contribute to the partnership.

Notes

8: Cash basis for small businesses

We have seen how to calculate the taxable trading profits for a business using the normal accruals method of accounting.

We now explore the differences for traders using the cash basis.

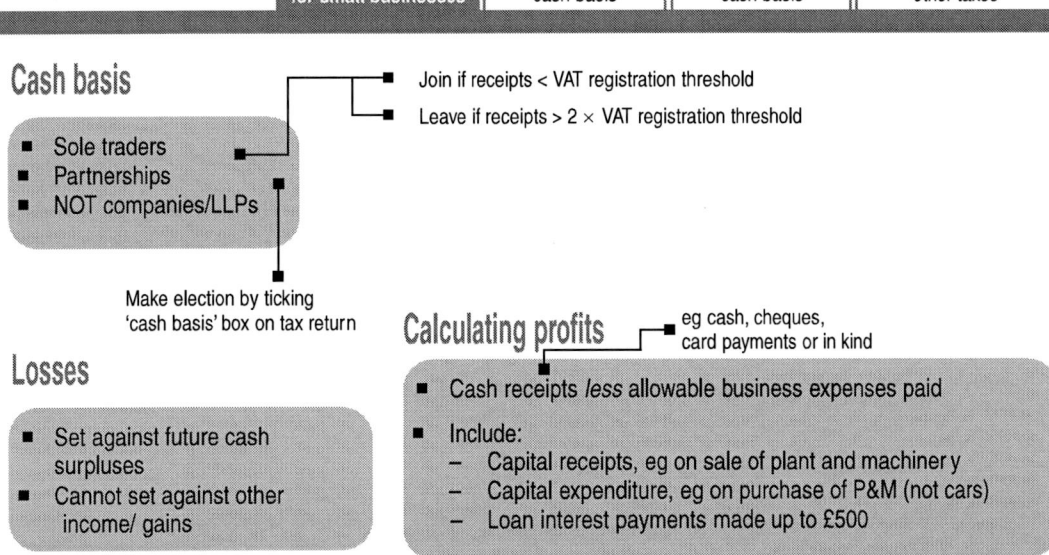

Cash basis

- Sole traders
- Partnerships
- NOT companies/LLPs

- Join if receipts < VAT registration threshold
- Leave if receipts > 2 × VAT registration threshold

Make election by ticking 'cash basis' box on tax return

Calculating profits

eg cash, cheques, card payments or in kind

- Cash receipts *less* allowable business expenses paid
- Include:
  - Capital receipts, eg on sale of plant and machinery
  - Capital expenditure, eg on purchase of P&M (not cars)
  - Loan interest payments made up to £500

Losses

- Set against future cash surpluses
- Cannot set against other income/ gains

New businesses

- Elect to join immediately
- Stay in scheme until:
  - Fails to meet criteria
  - Elects to use UK GAAP

Existing businesses

Adjustments required for:

- *Plant & machinery*
  - Deduction for part of TWDV b/f
  - Not for cars
- *Adjustment income/ expenditure*
  - Adjustment in 1st year
  - For income/ expenditure previously taxed/ allowed on accruals basis

Adjustments required on leaving scheme

Plant & machinery

- Unrelieved expenditure allocated to relevant pool
- eg HP asset where payments still due under agreeement

Adjustment income/ expenditure

- Similar to adjustments in existing business's 1st year
- Income:
  - Spread over 6 years
  - Tax as trading income
- Expenses:
  - Deductible in 1st period after leaves scheme

If partnership uses cash basis, no deduction for qualifying loan interest on loan:

- To invest in the partnership, or
- To buy P&M to be used in the partnership

Class 4 NICs are based on cash basis profits
▶▶ see later

Class 4 NIC

Interaction with other taxes

IT

- Must also use cash accounting scheme for VAT
- If shows VAT-inclusive figures in accounts must exclude VAT for tax purposes

VAT

CGT

Proceeds from sale of P&M:

- Taxable as trade receipt
- No capital gain
▶▶ see later

8: Cash basis for small businesses

Notes

9: Income tax for trusts

Topic List

Introduction

Interest in possession trusts

Discretionary trusts

When it comes to calculating income tax for a trust, we really only need to consider whether a trust is an interest in possession or a discretionary trust.

There are special income tax rules where a settlor retains an interest in a trust and when a beneficiary is a 'vulnerable' person.

Bare trust: Trustee is legal owner but beneficiary is absolutely entitled to property and its income

- Transparent for tax purposes
- Income taxed on beneficiary, not trustee

Interest in possession trust:

- Beneficiary (the 'life tenant') has right to receive income (an 'interest in possession')
- Capital passes to other beneficiary ('remainderman') when IIP comes to end

Discretionary trust:

- No beneficiary entitled to income or capital
- Up to discretion of the trustees which beneficiary benefits and how

Income is taxed on **trustee** first, then on the **beneficiary**

IIP trustees

- Calculate income in same way as for an individual, eg property income
- No:
  - Personal allowance
  - Bands of income
- No deduction for trust management expenses
- All income taxed at basic rates:
  - Non savings: 20%
  - Savings: 20%
  - Dividends: 10%
- Tax credits available for savings (20%) and dividend income (10%) as normal

Set expenses against dividend income first

IIP beneficiaries (life tenants)

- Entitled to trust's net income (ie after trust management expenses)
- Receive R185 statement of income showing net amount and tax credit
- Income retains its nature (eg rental income received by trust is taxed as rental income in beneficiary's hands)
- Taxed at beneficiary's rate(s)

Discretionary trustees

- Calculate income in same way as for an individual
- No:
  - Personal allowance
  - Bands of income
- **Can** deduct trust management expenses
- First £1,000 of income taxed at basic rate
- Rest of income taxed at trust rates:
  - NS/ Savings: 45%
  - Dividends: 37.5%
- Tax credits available for savings (20%) and dividend income (10%) as normal
- Tax pool shows tax credits available to cover income payments to beneficiaries

- Set expenses against dividend income first
- Gross up at appropriate **basic rate**

Beneficiaries

- Taxed only when receive income payment(s)
- Payments come with 45% tax credit
- Receive R185 statement of income showing net amount and tax credit
- Income always taxed as non-savings income
- Taxed at beneficiary's rate

- Tax non-savings income first, then savings income, then dividends

- If shortfall, trustees must pay extra tax to HMRC

10: Chargeable gains for individuals & trustees

This chapter reviews the basic principles of chargeable gains for individuals and trustees including chargeable and exempt persons, disposals and assets, how to compute simple gains and the charge to capital gains tax.

It also explains how to deal with part disposals, disposals to connected persons, disposal of chattels and how to apply principal private residence and lettings reliefs.

Chargeable persons, assets and disposals

Three elements are needed for a chargeable gain to arise.

1 A **chargeable person**: companies, individuals and partners are chargeable persons. ■———■ Charities and pension schemes are exempt from CGT

2 A **chargeable asset**: most assets wherever situated in the world are chargeable, but some assets are exempt. ■
Cars
Some chattels (eg racehorses)
Gilts
ISA investments

3 A **chargeable disposal**: this includes sales and gifts. Transfer of assets on death is not chargeable.

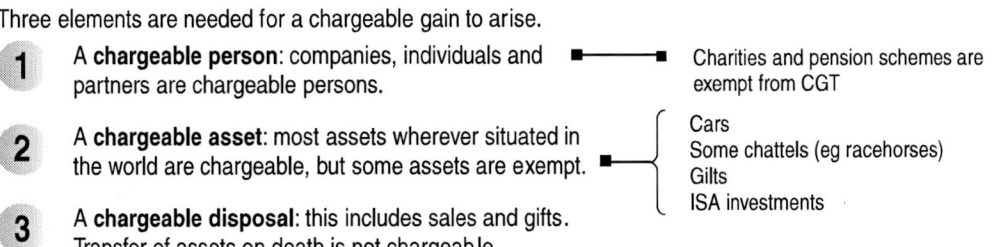

Computation

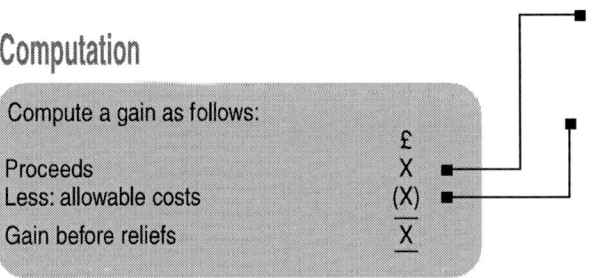

Compute a gain as follows:

	£
Proceeds	X
Less: allowable costs	(X)
Gain before reliefs	X

■ **Actual proceeds** or **market value** for disposals that are not bargains at arm's length (eg gifts)

■ Include:

(1) **Original cost** of the asset *or* **market value** if gifted *or* **probate value** if acquired on death

(2) **Enhancement expenditure** reflected in value of the asset at disposal

(3) **Incidental costs** of **acquisition** and **disposal** (eg legal fees)

Part disposals

On a part disposal, only take the relevant part of the cost of the asset into account.

$$\text{Cost} \times \frac{A}{A + B}$$

A = MV of part disposed of

B = MV of part kept

Costs relating to the part disposal are deductible in full

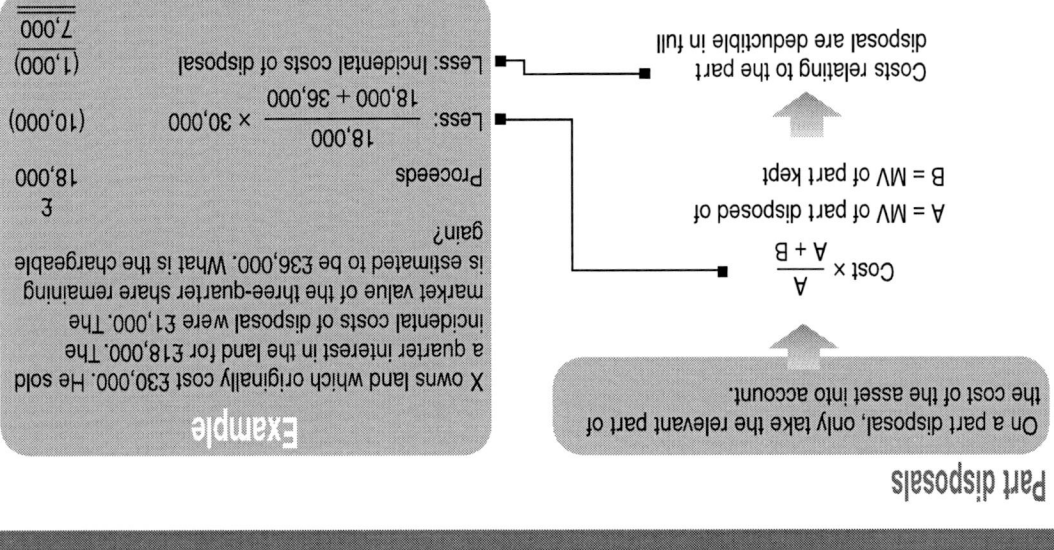

Example

X owns land which originally cost £30,000. He sold a quarter interest in the land for £18,000. The incidental costs of disposal were £1,000. The market value of the three-quarter share remaining is estimated to be £36,000. What is the chargeable gain?

	£
Proceeds	18,000
Less: $\dfrac{18,000}{18,000 + 36,000} \times 30,000$	(10,000)
Less: Incidental costs of disposal	(1,000)
	7,000

Annual exempt amount (AEA)

- *Individuals*: £10,900 (2013/14)
- *Trustees*: £5,450 (2013/14) ■
- Last deduction

Split between trusts created by same settlor (min £1,090)

Alert! Bare trusts are transparent for CGT purposes so gains on disposals of trust assets are taxed on the beneficiary not the trustees

Rates of CGT
– Individuals

- Taxed at 18% to the extent that the individual has any unused basic rate band (extended for gross Gift Aid donations and PPCs)
- Otherwise taxed at 28%

– Trustees

- Taxed at 28%

Spouses/civil partners

Transfers between them take place at no gain/no loss ie proceeds = cost

Connected persons

- Transfers between connected persons *(relatives, business partners, settlor of a trust and its trustees)* take place at market value

Trustees are also connected to anyone connected with the settlor

Pre-March 1982 assets

When an asset was acquired pre-March 1982 use MV82 figure NOT cost to calculate the gain.

	£
Proceeds	X
Less: 31.3.82 MV	(X)
Gain	X

Exam focus

You will be given the MV82 figure in the exam.

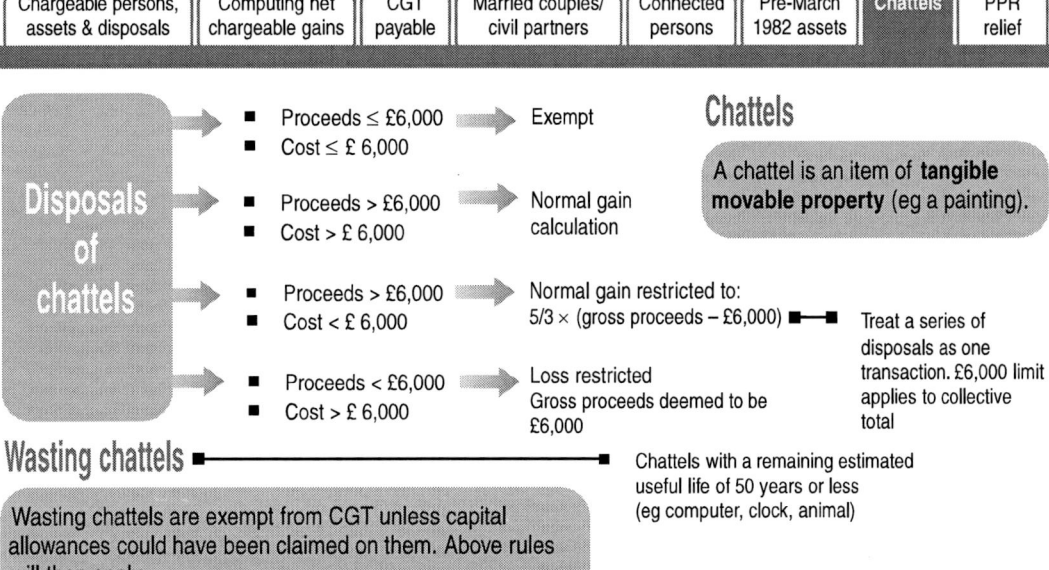

Disposals of chattels

- Proceeds ≤ £6,000
- Cost ≤ £6,000
→ Exempt

- Proceeds > £6,000
- Cost > £6,000
→ Normal gain calculation

- Proceeds > £6,000
- Cost < £6,000
→ Normal gain restricted to: 5/3 × (gross proceeds – £6,000) ▬■ Treat a series of disposals as one transaction. £6,000 limit applies to collective total

- Proceeds < £6,000
- Cost > £6,000
→ Loss restricted Gross proceeds deemed to be £6,000

Chattels

A chattel is an item of **tangible movable property** (eg a painting).

Wasting chattels ▬■ Chattels with a remaining estimated useful life of 50 years or less (eg computer, clock, animal)

Wasting chattels are exempt from CGT unless capital allowances could have been claimed on them. Above rules will then apply.

PPR relief

A gain on the disposal of a PPR is wholly exempt where the owner has occupied the whole residence throughout his period of ownership.

Where occupation has been for only part of a period, the proportion of the gain exempted is

$$\text{Total gain} \times \frac{\text{Period of occupation}}{\text{Total period of ownership}}$$

No relief for any business use

Periods of deemed occupation

- Absences of up to 3 years for any reason
- Absences while employed abroad
- Absences of up to 4 years while employed in UK

These periods must normally be preceded and followed by a period of actual occupation

- The last 36 months of ownership of a residence is always treated as a period of deemed occupation.

Provided that there is no other main residence at the time

- PPR relief is available for disposals of a trust property if a beneficiary has occupied it as his main residence.
- Trustee must make joint election with beneficiary

10: Chargeable gains for individuals and trustees

Second residence

- An individual is only allowed one PPR at a time. If he has two residences he can elect which one is to qualify.

  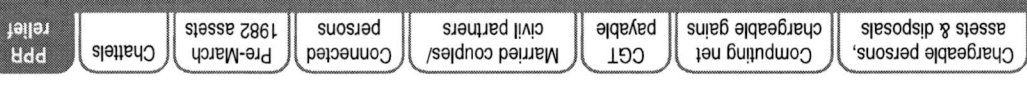

  Elect within 2 years of second property being used as a residence

- Spouses and civil partners must have the same PPR.

Letting exemption

A gain arising while a PPR is let is exempt up to the lowest of:

1. The amount of the PPR exemption
2. The gain in the let period
3. £40,000 (maximum)

Permitted area

The PPR exemption covers a house plus up to half a hectare of grounds. A larger area may be allowed depending on size and character of the house.

11: Shares and securities

Topic List

Disposals of shares and securities

Bonus and rights issues

This chapter deals with calculating gains on a disposal of shares by individuals and trustees which were acquired over a period of time, including the treatment of rights issues and bonus issues.

Matching rules

Disposals are matched with acquisitions in the following order.

- Same day acquisitions
- Acquisitions within the following 30 days on a FIFO basis
- s.104 pool

Computation

Same or next 30 days:
The computation is: proceeds less cost.

Exam focus

Learn the 'matching rules' because a crucial first step to getting a shares question right is to correctly match the shares sold to the original shares purchased.

Special rules apply to shares in the s.104 pool.

The s.104 pool

The s.104 pool is kept in 2 columns:

1 The **number** of shares

2 The **cost** (unless acquired before 31 March 1982, then MV 31.3.82)

On a disposal of some shares from the pool the cost is calculated on a pro-r ata basis.

The computation is: proceeds less cost.

Bonus issues

- Bonus issue shares are free shares
- Treated as acquired at same time as each holding
- Simply add the number of shares to the s.104 pool: there is no cost.

Rights issues

- Rights issue shares are purchased at below market value
- Treated as acquired on the same date as original holding
- Simply add the number of shares and cost of the rights shares to the s.104 pool.

Alert! Bonus and rights issue shares are only available to existing shareholders.

12: Leases

Topic List

Assignment of leases

Grant of leases

Ensure that you can distinguish between short and long leases and that you can deal with the CGT consequences of both sales of existing leases (ie assignments) and grants of new leases.

Assignment of a lease

Sale of existing interest

- **Long lease: more than 50 years to run**
  Ordinary disposal computation
- **Short lease: 50 years or less to run**
  Write down cost using table of percentages

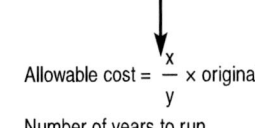

- Allowable cost = $\dfrac{x}{y}$ × original cost

  Number of years to run
  – when assigned = x
  – when acquired = y

- Percentages must be worked out to the nearest month, taking 1/12 of the difference between two adjacent figures in the table for each month

Example

Mr Miggles bought a 30 year lease on 1 June 2010 for £30,000. He assigned it on 1 June 2013 for £70,000. Compute the gain arising.

	£
Disposal proceeds	70,000
Less: £30,000 × $\dfrac{83.816}{87.330}$	(28,793)
	41,207

% (27) = 83.816   % (30) = 87.330

Grant of a lease

Owner/ landlord creates a new lease for a tenant to occupy the property

- **Long lease: grant lease of > 50 years**

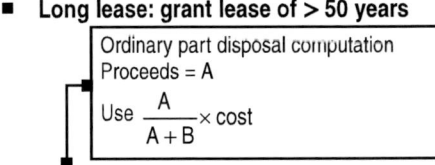

Ordinary part disposal computation
Proceeds = A

Use $\dfrac{A}{A+B} \times$ cost

A = premium
B = value of remainder (reversionary interest)

- **Short lease: grants lease of ≤ 50 years**

$$\dfrac{x-y}{z} \times \text{cost}$$

x = % years left on grant of sub lease
y = % years left when sub lease expires
z = % years left when lease acquired

- a = capital element of premium P $\times \dfrac{(n-1)}{50}$

Out of the freehold or original lease >50yrs
Modified part disposal computation
Proceeds = a

Use $\dfrac{a}{A+B} \times$ cost

Out of original lease ≤ 50yrs
Ordinary part disposal computation
Proceeds = A (full premium)
Use lease percentage table to apportion cost
Deduct property income assessment from the gain

Notes

13: Overseas aspects of income tax & CGT

Topic List

Residence and domicile

Overseas aspects of income tax

Overseas aspects of capital gains tax

In this chapter we look at the overseas aspects of income tax and capital gains tax and make sure you understand the meaning of the terms residence and domicile, and their significance.

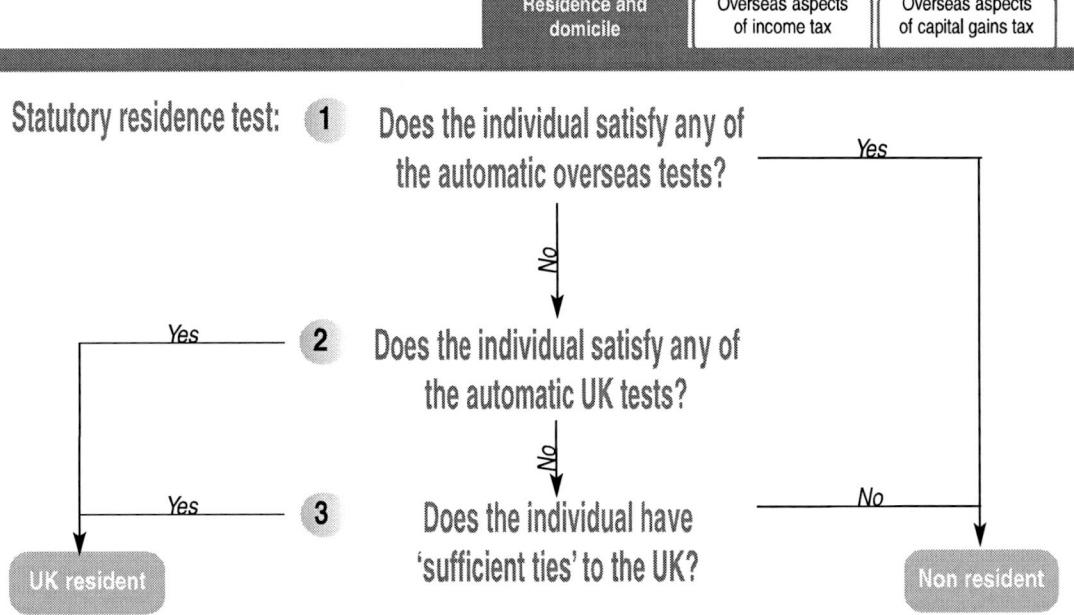

Statutory residence test:

1 Does the individual satisfy any of the automatic overseas tests? — Yes → Non resident

No ↓

2 Does the individual satisfy any of the automatic UK tests? — Yes → UK resident

No ↓

3 Does the individual have 'sufficient ties' to the UK? — Yes → UK resident — No → Non resident

Automatic overseas tests

- Resident in one of last 3 years and spends < 16 days in UK
- Not resident in any of last 3 years and spends < 46 days in UK
- Works full-time overseas

Automatic UK tests

- Spends at least 183 days in UK
- Period of $\geq$ 91 consecutive days during which:
  - Has home in the UK, and
  - Has no home overseas (ignore home(s) he visits for < 30 days in tax year)
- Works full-time in UK

Ties

- Family
- Accommodation
- Work
- 90 days
- More time in the UK than elsewhere?

■ Only consider final tie if was resident in at least one of the three previous tax years

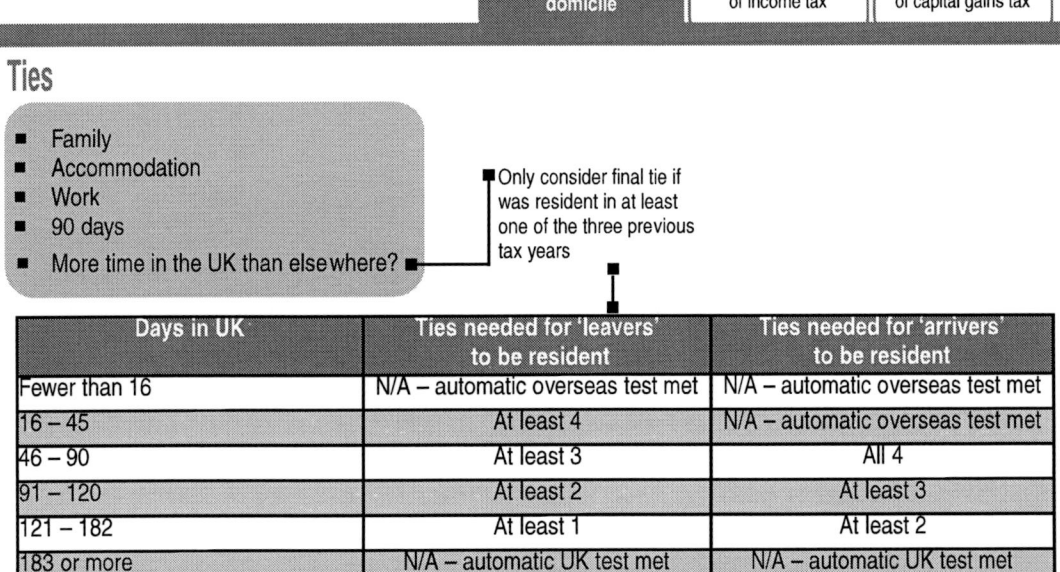

Days in UK	Ties needed for 'leavers' to be resident	Ties needed for 'arrivers' to be resident
Fewer than 16	N/A – automatic overseas test met	N/A – automatic overseas test met
16 – 45	At least 4	N/A – automatic overseas test met
46 – 90	At least 3	All 4
91 – 120	At least 2	At least 3
121 – 182	At least 1	At least 2
183 or more	N/A – automatic UK test met	N/A – automatic UK test met

Domicile

- Country of permanent home
- Three main types of domicile:
  - Origin
  - Dependency
  - Choice

- Deemed domicile applies for IHT only ▸▸ see later

UK resident but non-UK domiciled individuals can claim to be taxed on overseas income only when it is **remitted** to the UK

ie '**remittance basis**'

Can only change domicile by:

- Severing ties with the old country, and
- Establishing a permanent life in the new country

Employment income

1 Resident and domiciled in UK ➡ Taxable on **worldwide** earnings

2 Resident but not domiciled ➡
- Taxable on **worldwide** earnings in UK
- BUT may claim **remittance** basis for overseas earnings if either:
  - **1** Overseas duties for non-UK resident employer, or
  - **2** Was not resident for any 3 consecutive years out of previous 5 tax years

'Chargeable overseas earnings' ■——■

3 Not resident in UK ➡
- UK earnings taxed in UK
- Foreign earnings **not** taxable

Tax free overseas employment expenses

- Overseas board and lodgings

- Any number of visits home

- Travel costs for up to two return visits of spouse and minor children if period of absence at least 60 continuous days

Other income

- **Foreign dividends** – taxed in the same way as UK dividends (ie notional 10% tax credit if company pays overseas equivalent of corporation tax)

- **Overseas interest** – taxed in the same way as UK savings income

- **Overseas trade** – profits calculated as for UK trade

- **Overseas rental income** – taxed in same way as UK rental income (cannot be a FHL if outside EEA)

Taxed on **arising** basis unless the **remittance** basis applies, ie if the individual is not domiciled in the UK

If remittance basis applies, all income, including dividends and interest, is taxed as **non-savings** income.

Foreign pension

- If taxed on arising basis: 90% taxable

- If taxed on remittance basis: 100% taxable when brought into UK

Remittance basis

Income taxed only when brought into the UK

If individual is:

- Non-UK domiciled, and
- Has foreign income

Foreign income taxed on arising basis unless remittance basis claimed.

Remittance basis **automatically** applies if the individual has:

- Unremitted income/gains in tax year < £2,000, or

- No UK gains and UK investment income ≤ £100 which has been taxed in the UK *and* makes no remittances in the tax year *and* either aged < 18 or been resident in UK for not more than 6 years out of last 9.

If remittance basis is **claimed**:
- No personal allowance
- £30,000 RBC if UK resident for ≥ 7 years out of previous 9 tax years *and* aged >18 years

Increases to £50,000 when resident for ≥ 12 out of previous 14 tax years

13: Overseas aspects of income tax & CGT

Double tax relief is given to prevent income being taxed in both the UK and overseas

1 Agreements

Relief may be given under an agreement between the two countries.

If no agreement:

2 Credit relief

- Foreign income brought into the tax computation gross
- Treated as the *top slice* of individual's income.
- Relief = lower of:
  (i) The foreign tax, and
  (ii) The UK tax
- Deduct from the UK tax.

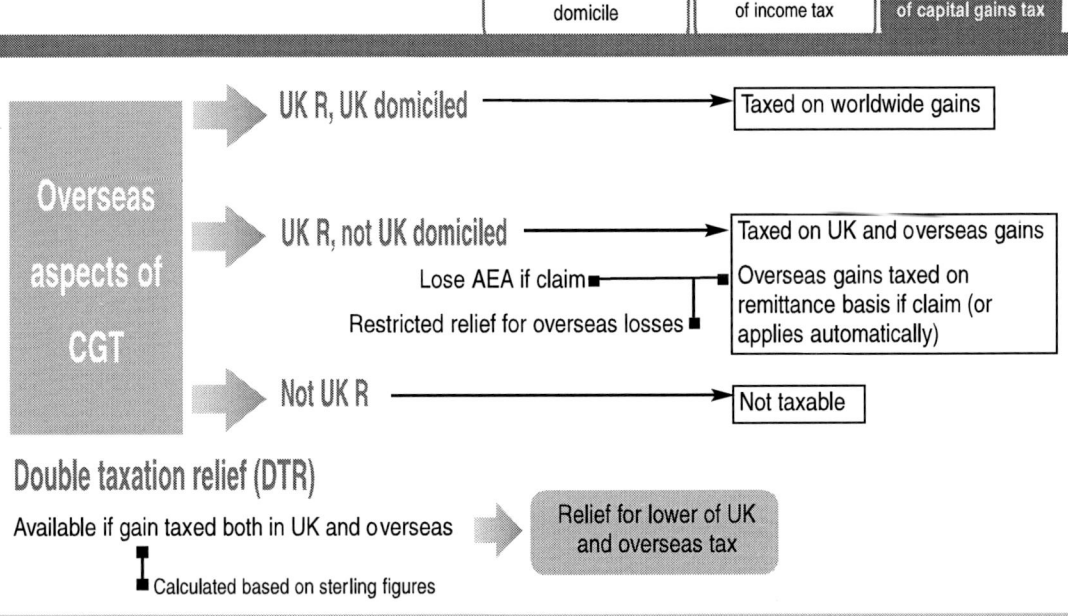

Overseas aspects of CGT

UK R, UK domiciled → Taxed on worldwide gains

UK R, not UK domiciled → Taxed on UK and overseas gains

Lose AEA if claim ■

Restricted relief for overseas losses ■

Overseas gains taxed on remittance basis if claim (or applies automatically)

Not UK R → Not taxable

Double taxation relief (DTR)

Available if gain taxed both in UK and overseas → Relief for lower of UK and overseas tax

■ Calculated based on sterling figures

Notes

14: NIC and administration

This chapter reviews the basic principles of National Insurance Contributions (NICs).

It then extends your knowledge to Class 1A and Class 1B contributions payable by employers, NICs on company directors and the principles of annual maximum contributions.

It also deals with an additional self assessment topic – reduction of payments on account.

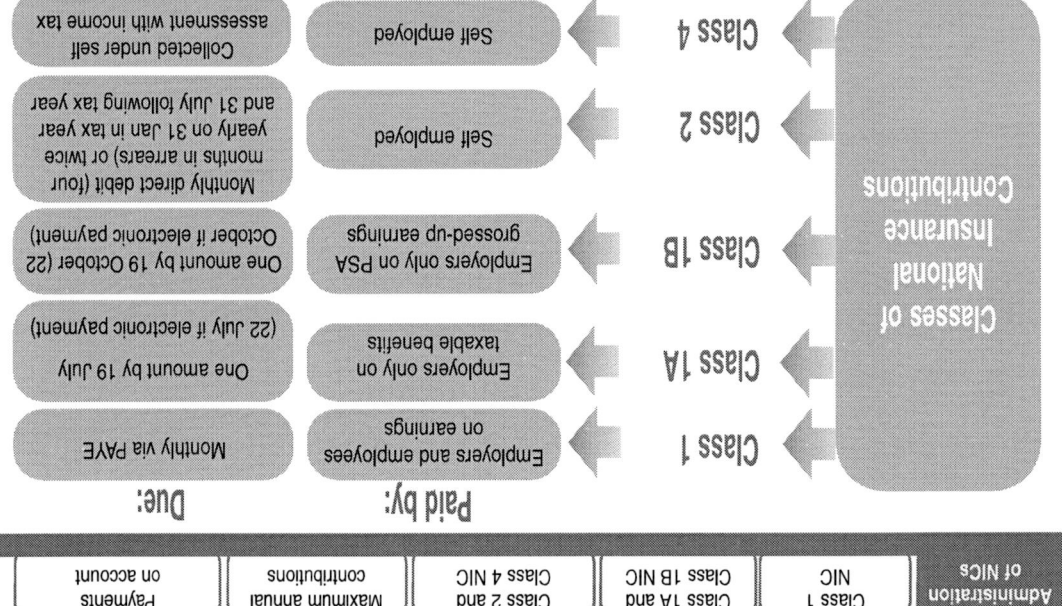

Classes of National Insurance Contributions

	Paid by:	Due:
Class 1	Employers and employees on earnings	Monthly via PAYE
Class 1A	Employers only on taxable benefits	One amount by 19 July (22 July if electronic payment)
Class 1B	Employers only on PSA grossed-up earnings	One amount by 19 October (22 October if electronic payment)
Class 2	Self employed	Monthly direct debit (four months in arrears) or twice yearly on 31 Jan in tax year and 31 July following tax year
Class 4	Self employed	Collected under self assessment with income tax

Administration of NICs

| Class 1 NIC | Class 1A and Class 1B NIC | Class 2 and Class 4 NIC | Maximum annual contributions | Payments on account |

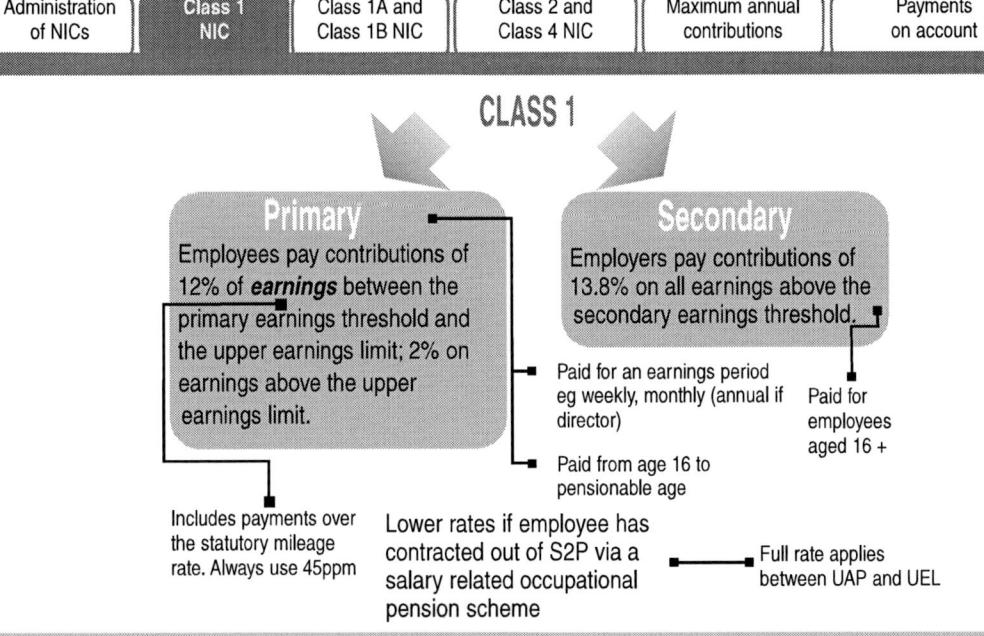

CLASS 1

Primary

Employees pay contributions of 12% of *earnings* between the primary earnings threshold and the upper earnings limit; 2% on earnings above the upper earnings limit.

Secondary

Employers pay contributions of 13.8% on all earnings above the secondary earnings threshold.

Paid for an earnings period eg weekly, monthly (annual if director)

Paid for employees aged 16 +

Paid from age 16 to pensionable age

Includes payments over the statutory mileage rate. Always use 45ppm

Lower rates if employee has contracted out of S2P via a salary related occupational pension scheme

Full rate applies between UAP and UEL

CLASS 1A

Employers pay Class 1A contributions at 13.8% on most **taxable benefits** provided to their employees.

CLASS 1B

Payable by employers at 13.8% on the grossed-up value of earnings included in a **PAYE settlement agreement (PSA)**.

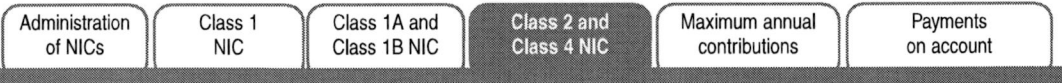

The self employed (ie sole traders and partners) pay Class 2 *and* Class 4 NICs.

Class 2

Class 2 are paid at a flat weekly rate. ▪━━━ ■ No contributions are payable if the individual's accounts profits are below the small earnings exception

■ Profits are the tax adjusted profits

Class 4

Class 4 NICs are 9% of any profits falling between an upper and lower profits limit and 2% above upper profits limit.

14: NIC and administration

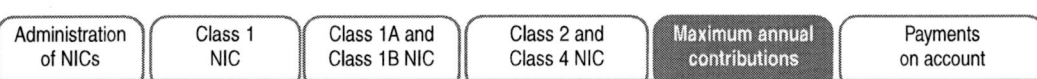

Maximum annual contributions

Deferment available if:
- More than one employment, or
- Paying both Classes 1 and 2 (ie employed and self employed).

Annual maximum NIC limit if paying Classes 1, 2 and 4.

Payment of tax

Interest (but no penalty) due if late

Payments on account (POA) of income tax and Class 4 NICs must be made by 31 January in tax year and by the following 31 July.

Each POA is 50% of the previous tax year's income tax and Class 4 NIC liability less tax suffered at source

Can reduce if lower liability than previous year expected

No POAs if previous year's tax paid under self assessment was:

- <£1,000, or
- <20% of the total income tax and Class 4 liability

Notes

15: IHT – basic principles

Topic List

Scope of Inheritance Tax (IHT)

Exempt transfers

Lifetime transfers

This chapter explains how to calculate the value of a transfer for IHT purposes, after deducting available exemptions.

It also shows how to calculate the tax payable on lifetime gifts both when made, and on the death of the donor, taking account of taper relief.

IHT can only arise if there is a **transfer of value**.

Transfer of value

A gratuitous disposition which results in a reduction of a person's net worth.

Diminution in value

The value of a gift is always the loss to the donor. This is the **diminution in value principle.**

Property outside the UK owned by persons domiciled abroad

Trusts

IHT is often charged when someone (the **settlor**) sets up a trust (or **settlement**) by giving assets to **trustees** to hold on behalf of **beneficiaries**

Exceptions to the IHT charge

Transfers:
1. Where there is no gratuitous intent, or
2. Made in the course of a trade, or
3. For family maintenance, or
4. Of **excluded property**

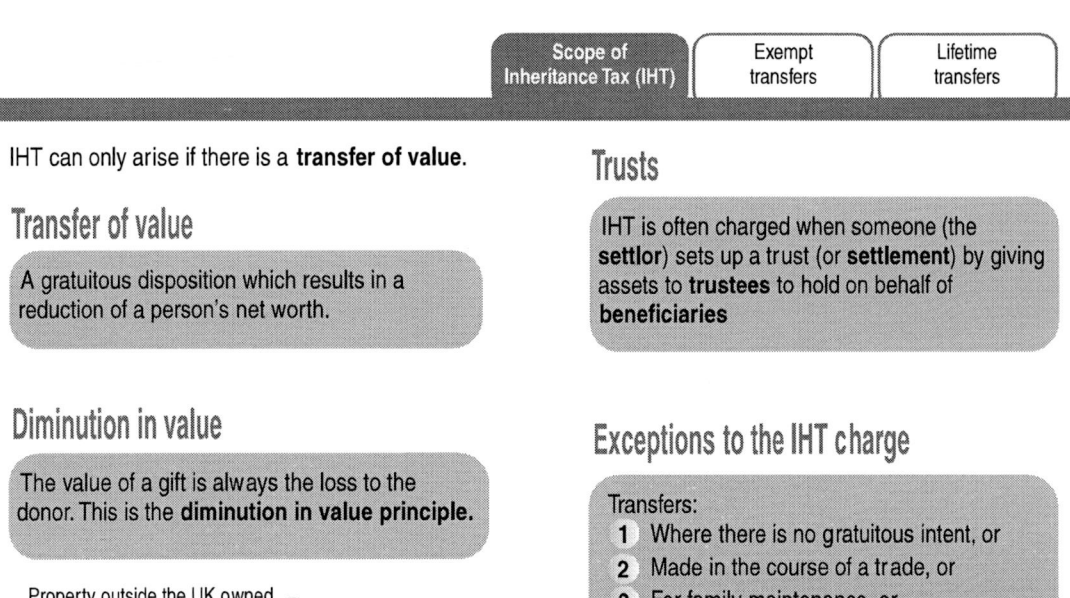

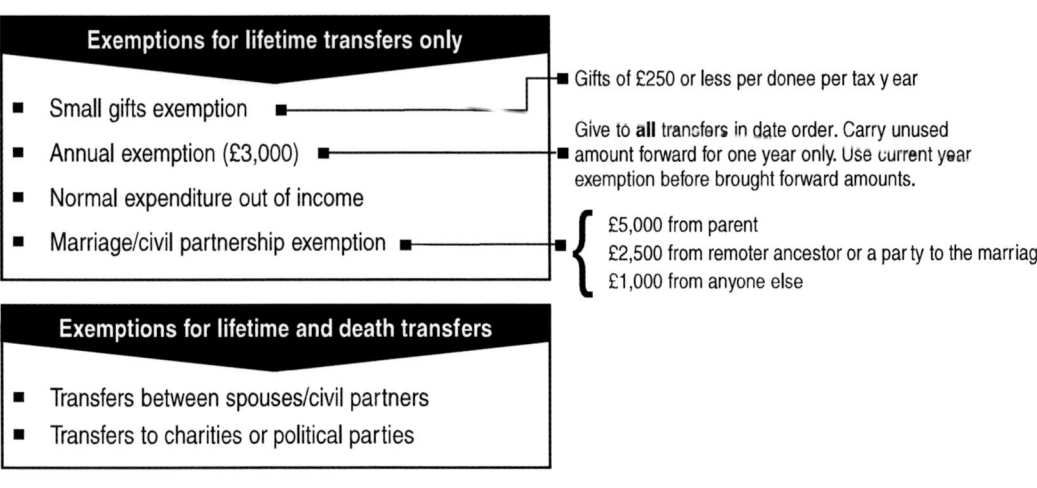

Exemptions for lifetime transfers only

- Small gifts exemption ■ ──────■ Gifts of £250 or less per donee per tax year

- Annual exemption (£3,000) ■ ──────■ Give to **all** transfers in date order. Carry unused amount forward for one year only. Use current year exemption before brought forward amounts.

- Normal expenditure out of income

- Marriage/civil partnership exemption ■ ───┤ £5,000 from parent
    £2,500 from remoter ancestor or a party to the marriage
    £1,000 from anyone else

Exemptions for lifetime and death transfers

- Transfers between spouses/civil partners
- Transfers to charities or political parties

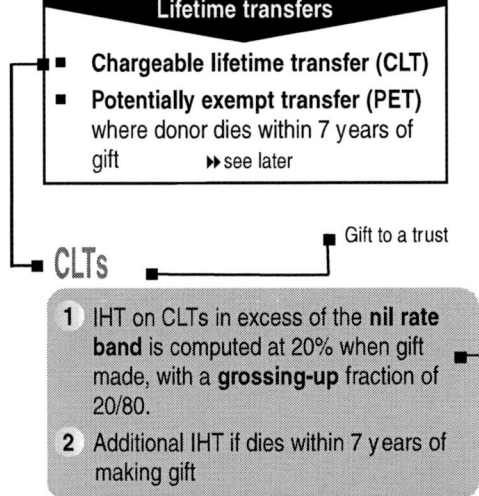

Lifetime transfers

- **Chargeable lifetime transfer (CLT)**
- **Potentially exempt transfer (PET)** where donor dies within 7 years of gift ⤳ see later

CLTs

Gift to a trust

1. IHT on CLTs in excess of the **nil rate band** is computed at 20% when gift made, with a **grossing-up** fraction of 20/80.
2. Additional IHT if dies within 7 years of making gift

Grossing up is needed if the donor pays the IHT, because he has lost both the amount transferred and the tax.

Exam focus

When you have grossed up a transfer, you can check your figures by computing the tax and the net transfer from the gross transfer.

Nil rate band

IHT charged at 0% on **£325,000** (2013/14)

Additional tax due on death

The IHT on each **lifetime transfer** made in the 7 years before death is found as follows:

1. All chargeable transfers (including **PETs** which have become chargeable) in the 7 years before the transfer in question use up the nil rate band.
2. Find the tax at full rates (0% and 40%), then deduct any taper relief.
3. Deduct any tax already paid on the transfer (CLTs only - no repayment available).

■ Transfers remain in the cumulation and use the nil band for 7 years, then they drop out

■ A % reduction in the IHT charge is given if the transfer was made more than 3 years before death

PETs

■ Gifts between individuals.
■ Gifts to certain interest in possession trusts and A&M trusts before 22 March 2006

■ Exempt during donor's lifetime
■ Fully exempt if survives 7 years from gift
■ IHT if dies within 7 years of making gift

Fall in value relief

If at date of donor's death a gifted asset has either:

1 Been sold for less than its MV when originally gifted

OR

2 Is still held but is worth less than its MV when originally gifted

Deduct 'fall in value' from gross chargeable transfer (GCT)

Alert! Fall in value relief only affects the calculation of tax for the donee. It does NOT affect the donor's cumulative total.

16: IHT – death estate and valuation

Topic List

IHT on the death estate

Valuation

This chapter deals with the IHT payable on an individual's death estate after taking account of reliefs and exemptions and using the special valuation rules for certain assets.

Death estate

The death estate includes
1. The free estate ■————————■ Assets owned outright
2. Settled property

■ Property in a qualifying interest in possession (IIP) trust where the deceased was the life tenant

Debts ■——■ eg accrued rent payable to date of death, outstanding loans, etc

- Deduct debt from asset debt relates to, eg mortgage is deducted from the property it was taken out on
- Only deduct if remains unpaid for commercial reason and not to obtain a tax advantage
- No deduction if debt incurred to acquire **'excluded property'**

■ ie foreign assets of non-doms

Other liabilities

Can deduct:
- Taxes to date of death
- Reasonable funeral expenses ■——■ Including tombstone

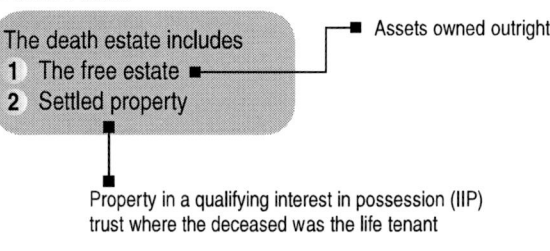

Calculating death tax

1 Calculate total value of estate (probate value less liabilities) ■━━━━━━━━━ ■ Market value at date of death

2 Nil rate band is used by chargeable transfers in last 7 years ■━━━━━━━━━ ■ CLTs and PETs that have become chargeable
Remaining nil band @ 0% ■━━━━━━━

■ Increase nil rate band by proportion equal to unused proportion of nil rate band of deceased spouse(s)/civil partner(s) up to a maximum of 100%

3 Balance of estate @ 40% (36% if 10% or more of net estate given to charity)
Deduct quick succession relief (QSR) ▶▶ see below

Quick succession relief (QSR)

QSR is given when someone dies within five years of receiving property in a chargeable transfer (the first transfer).

→ QSR is deducted from the IHT on the estate.

Computation

1. Take the tax paid on the first transfer, and multiply it by the net transfer/the gross transfer

2. Then multiply the result by a percentage, from 100% (for a gap of one year or less) to 20% (for a gap of more than four years)

Period between transfers	% relief
1 yr or less	100
1 – 2 yrs	80
2 – 3 yrs	60
3 – 4 yrs	40
4 – 5 yrs	20
> 5 yrs	0

Assets are generally valued at their open market values.

Diminution in value

Value before transfer	X
Value left with after transfer	(X)
Transfer of value	X

Related property

Related property includes:

1. Property owned by the transferor's spouse
2. Property which the transferor or his spouse gave to a charity or political party in an exempt transfer, if the recipient has owned the property within the preceding five years

Related property is taken into account if doing so increases the value of assets

16: IHT – death estate and valuation

Special valuation rules

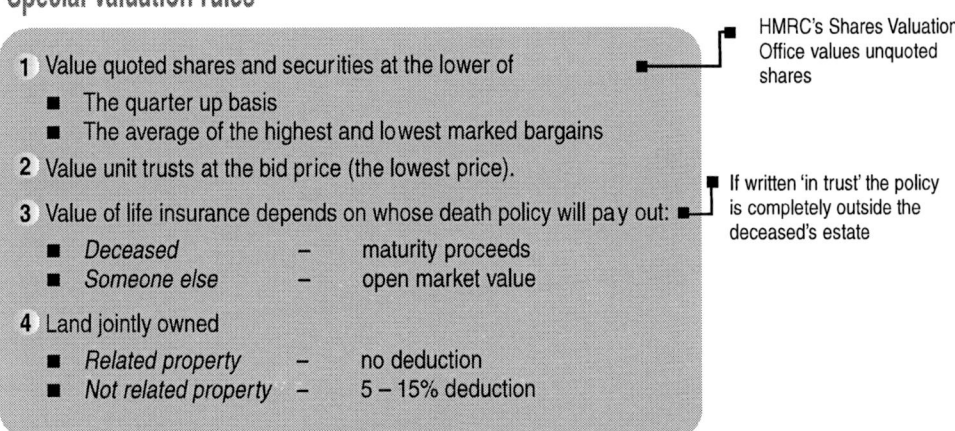

1 Value quoted shares and securities at the lower of
  - The quarter up basis
  - The average of the highest and lowest marked bargains

HMRC's Shares Valuation Office values unquoted shares

2 Value unit trusts at the bid price (the lowest price).

3 Value of life insurance depends on whose death policy will pay out:

If written 'in trust' the policy is completely outside the deceased's estate

  - *Deceased* – maturity proceeds
  - *Someone else* – open market value

4 Land jointly owned
  - *Related property* – no deduction
  - *Not related property* – 5 – 15% deduction

17: IHT – other aspects

This chapter deals with the overseas aspects of IHT and the administration provisions for IHT.

Deemed domicile

Treat as UK domiciled for IHT purposes only:

- If resident in the UK for 17 out of 20 tax years,
- For 36 months after ceases to be UK domiciled

- UK domiciled – IHT on all assets wherever situated
- Non-UK domiciled – IHT only on UK assets

Double tax relief

DTR is available if property is situated overseas and suffers a foreign equivalent of IHT.

- DTR is the lower of the UK IHT on the asset (at the average rate) and the foreign tax.
- The DTR is deducted from the IHT.

Location of assets

- Immovable property – where situated
- Debts – where debtor resident
- Registered shares – where registered
- Bearer shares – where certificate kept
- Bank account – where branch situated
- Goodwill – where business carried on

Transfers between spouses/ civil partners

- Both UK domiciled: Completely exempt
- To non-UK domiciled spouse/CP: Exemption **limited** to value of nil rate band

Applies for IHT only (not IT or CGT) ■——■ **UK domicile election**

- Non-UK domiciled spouse/CP can make a UK domicile election
- Spouse exemption = unlimited
- But brings all overseas assets within scope of UK IHT

Accounts

By end of 12 m after gift for:
CLT delivered by donor

By end of 12 m after death for:
PET delivered by donee
Death estate delivered by PRs

■ No account needed for excepted transfers or estates

Interest runs from six months after the end of the month of death

Due date

1. Lifetime IHT on a CLT is due on the later of
   (i) 30 April after the end of the tax year of transfer
   (ii) Six months after the end of the month of transfer
2. IHT due on CLTs/PETs as a result of death is due six months after the month of death.
3. The due date for IHT on the free estate is the date of delivery of the account.

Instalment payments

- IHT on certain property can be paid in ten equal annual instalments on CLTs where tax is borne by the donee, or on the death estate.
- Additionally, IHT due on PETs as a result of the death of the donor can be paid in instalments.

Land and buildings
Most unquoted shares and securities
Business/interest in business

Penalties

For an account submitted late:

■ Initial fixed penalty	£100
■ Between three and six months late	daily fixed penalty of £10 for maximum of 90 days
■ Between six and twelve months late	5% of tax due (min £300)
■ Over twelve months late	5% of tax due (min £300)

- For late payment of IHT:
  5% penalties of tax unpaid on filing date then 6 months and 12 months from filing date

Notes

18: Corporation tax

Topic List

Charge to corporation tax

Taxable total profits

Computation of corporation tax

Administration of corporation tax

This chapter builds on your basic knowledge of corporation tax by covering computation of taxable total profits for long periods of account.

It then looks at more complex situations for the computation of CT, eg dealing with associated companies and where an accounting period falls within more than one financial year.

Finally, it considers the administrative implications of a company having a long period of account and payment of corporation tax instalments for a short accounting period.

Residence

A UK resident company is chargeable on its worldwide profits. A company is resident in the UK if it is incorporated in the UK or if its central management and control are in the UK.

Alert! An accounting period can never be > 12 months.

If a company prepares accounts for a longer period, it must be split into 2 CT accounting periods.

1st 12 months form the 1st accounting period

Remaining months form the 2nd accounting period

Period of account

A period of account is the period for which accounts are prepared.

Accounting period

An accounting period is the period for which corporation tax is charged.

- Begins when the company starts to trade, acquires a source of income or immediately after the end of the previous accounting period.

- Ends 12 months after it starts, when the period of account ends, when it starts or ceases to trade or when it ceases to be UK resident.

Taxable total profits

A company's **taxable total profits** are arrived at by adding together its various sources of income and chargeable gains and then deducting qualifying donations.

Proforma for calculating taxable total profits

	£
Trading income	X
Non-trading loan relationships	X
Miscellaneous income	X
Property income	X
Chargeable gains	X
Total profits	X
Qualifying donations	(X)
Taxable total profits	X

Profits of trades ■ ──── ■ Trading income

Interest from non-trading loan relationships ■ ──── ■ Non-trading loan relationships
(eg bank/building society interest)

Any income not otherwise charged ■ ──── ■ Miscellaneous income

Income from property in the UK ■ ──── ■ Property income

Donations paid in the accounting period ■ ──── ■ Qualifying donations

Alert! Exempt dividends from other UK and overseas companies are not included in taxable total profits.

18: Corporation tax

Certain items of expenditure is **allowable** (ie can be deducted) when calculating taxable total profits

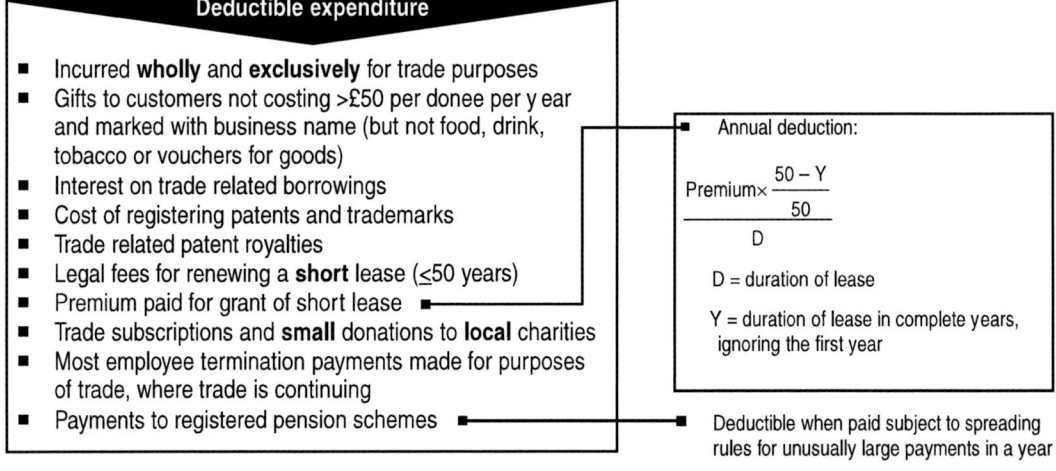

Deductible expenditure

- Incurred **wholly** and **exclusively** for trade purposes
- Gifts to customers not costing >£50 per donee per year and marked with business name (but not food, drink, tobacco or vouchers for goods)
- Interest on trade related borrowings
- Cost of registering patents and trademarks
- Trade related patent royalties
- Legal fees for renewing a **short** lease (≤50 years)
- Premium paid for grant of short lease
- Trade subscriptions and **small** donations to **local** charities
- Most employee termination payments made for purposes of trade, where trade is continuing
- Payments to registered pension schemes

- Annual deduction:

$$\text{Premium} \times \frac{\dfrac{50 - Y}{50}}{D}$$

  D = duration of lease

  Y = duration of lease in complete years, ignoring the first year

- Deductible when paid subject to spreading rules for unusually large payments in a year

For a long period of account, divide profits between the accounting periods as follows:

Division of profits		
	Trading income	Time apportion amount before CAs
	CAs	Compute separately for each period
	Property income	Time apportionment
	Investment income	Time apportion on accruals basis
	Miscellaneous income	Time apportion on accruals basis
	Gains	Allocate to period of disposal
	Qualifying donations	Allocate to period in which paid

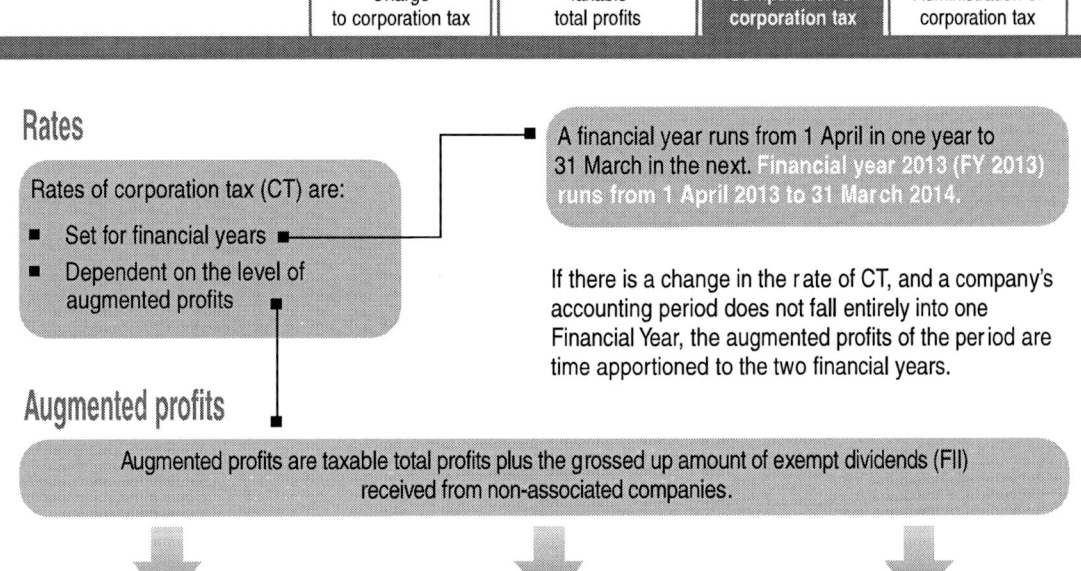

Rates

Rates of corporation tax (CT) are:

- Set for financial years
- Dependent on the level of augmented profits

A financial year runs from 1 April in one year to 31 March in the next. Financial year 2013 (FY 2013) runs from 1 April 2013 to 31 March 2014.

If there is a change in the rate of CT, and a company's accounting period does not fall entirely into one Financial Year, the augmented profits of the period are time apportioned to the two financial years.

Augmented profits

Augmented profits are taxable total profits plus the grossed up amount of exempt dividends (FII) received from non-associated companies.

The **main rate** (FY 2013 – 23%) of CT applies if augmented profits exceed the CT upper limit.

The **small profits rate** (FY 2013 – 20%) applies if augmented profits are below the CT lower limit

Marginal relief is given if augmented profits fall between the CT upper and lower limits

Marginal relief formula

Standard fraction × (Upper limit – Augmented profits) × $\dfrac{\text{Taxable total profits}}{\text{Augmented profits}}$

Upper and lower limits

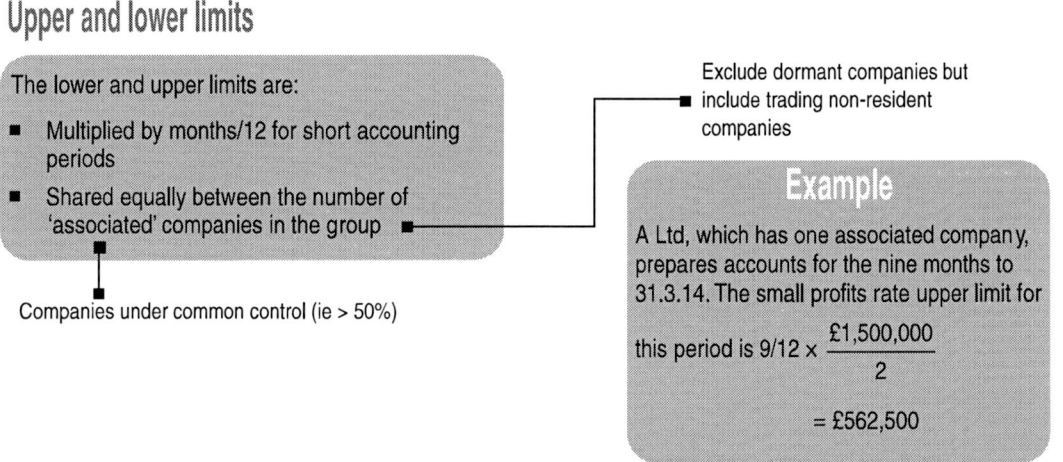

The lower and upper limits are:

- Multiplied by months/12 for short accounting periods
- Shared equally between the number of 'associated' companies in the group

Companies under common control (ie > 50%)

Exclude dormant companies but include trading non-resident companies

Example

A Ltd, which has one associated company, prepares accounts for the nine months to 31.3.14. The small profits rate upper limit for

this period is $9/12 \times \dfrac{£1,500,000}{2}$

$= £562,500$

Returns

A company must normally file its CT return (CT600) by the due filing date which is the later of:

- 12 months after the end of each period to which the return relates
- 3 months after a notice requiring the return was issued

Payment

Any company that pays CT at the main rate

'Large' companies must pay their anticipated CT liability in quarterly instalments.

- Due 14th of the month

Penalties

- *Late return:* fixed penalty = £100
- *>3 months late:* daily fixed penalty of £10 for maximum of 90 days
- *6 - 12 months late:* tax geared penalty = 5% of the tax due
- *>12 months late:* tax geared penalty = further 5% of the tax due
- Tax geared penalties are subject to minimum of £300

- *12 month AP:*
  Instalments due in:
  - months 7 and 10 of the period
  - months 1 and 4 of the following period
- *AP < 12 (n) months:*
  - each instalment = $3 \times CT/n$
  - instalments due at 3 monthly intervals
  - final instalment in month 4 of the following period

Notes

19: Chargeable gains for companies

This chapter deals with calculating chargeable gains for companies.

A key area is the rules for the disposal of shares and securities, including recognising when an exemption applies.

Computation

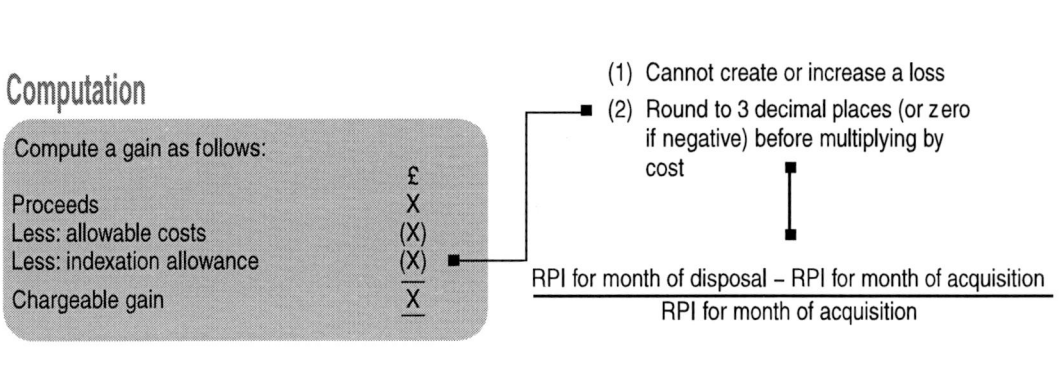

Compute a gain as follows:

	£
Proceeds	X
Less: allowable costs	(X)
Less: indexation allowance	(X)
Chargeable gain	X

(1) Cannot create or increase a loss

(2) Round to 3 decimal places (or zero if negative) before multiplying by cost

$$\frac{\text{RPI for month of disposal} - \text{RPI for month of acquisition}}{\text{RPI for month of acquisition}}$$

When an asset was acquired before 31 March 1982, need a two column computation:

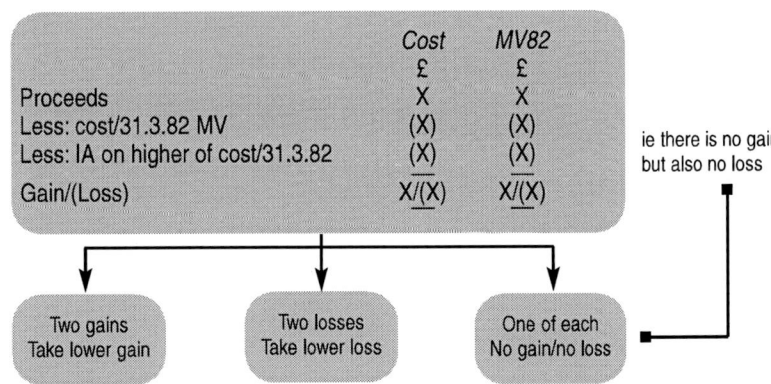

Exam focus

You will be given the MV82 figure in the exam.

	Cost	*MV82*
	£	£
Proceeds	X	X
Less: cost/31.3.82 MV	(X)	(X)
Less: IA on higher of cost/31.3.82	(X)	(X)
Gain/(Loss)	X/(X)	X/(X)

ie there is no gain but also no loss

Two gains
Take lower gain

Two losses
Take lower loss

One of each
No gain/no loss

If makes a '31 March 1982 MV' election, only need one calculation using 31.3.82 MV.

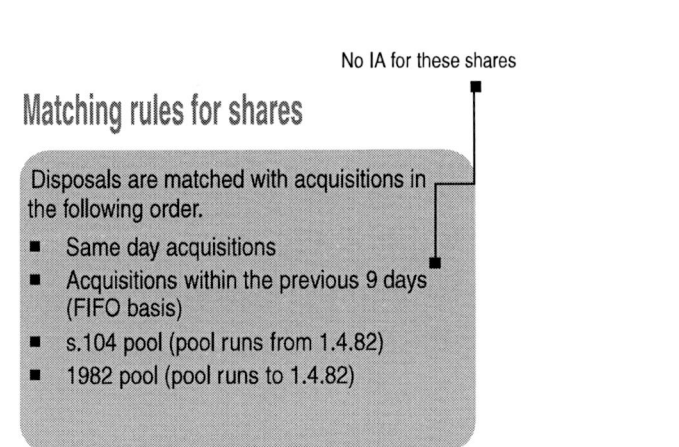

No IA for these shares

Matching rules for shares

Disposals are matched with acquisitions in the following order.

- Same day acquisitions
- Acquisitions within the previous 9 days (FIFO basis)
- s.104 pool (pool runs from 1.4.82)
- 1982 pool (pool runs to 1.4.82)

The s.104 pool

The s.104 pool is kept in 3 columns:

1 The **number** of shares

2 The **cost**

3 The **indexed cost**

On a disposal of some shares from the pool, the cost and indexed cost are calculated on a pro-rata basis.

The computation is: proceeds less cost less IA.

The IA is the excess of the indexed cost over the cost. It cannot increase or create a loss.

The indexation factor in this pool is NOT rounded to 3 decimal places.

The 1982 pool

The 1982 pool has 3 columns:

1 The **number** of shares

2 The **cost**

3 The **31 March 1982** market value

On a disposal of some shares from the pool, the cost and MV82 are calculated on a pro-rata basis.

The computation is: proceeds less cost less IA.

Calculate IA separately
(indexation factor rounded to 3 decimal places).

Alert! Bonus issue and rights shares are only available to existing shareholders.

Bonus issues

- Bonus issue shares are free shares
- Treated as acquired at same time as each holding
- Simply add the number of shares to each holding as there is no cost to add to the 1982 pool, s.104 pool etc

Rights issues

- Rights issue shares are purchased at below market value
- Treated as acquired at same time as each holding
- Add the number of shares and cost of the rights shares to each holding, ie to the 1982 pool, s.104 pool etc
- Indexation:
  - *s.104 pool:* Index to date of the rights issue
  - *1982 pool:* Separate IA calculation needed

Substantial shareholding exemption

1. Trading company owns 10% or more in another trading company

2. For 12 months over a two year period

3. Gain on sale of shares is exempt (loss is not allowable)

Notes

20: Additional aspects of corporation tax

Topic List

Pension contributions

Loan relationships

Intangible fixed assets

Research and development expenditure

Property income

Double taxation relief

This chapter deals with the treatment of large pension contributions to employees' pensions, loan relationships, intangible assets owned by a company, research and development expenditure, the taxation of property income and double tax relief.

Employer pension contributions

- Contributions paid by employer are allowable trading expense in period **paid**
- No limit but spreading provisions apply for **large contributions** ■

■ Current period contribution > 210% × amount paid in previous period and

■ Amount exceeding 110% × amount paid in previous period (the 'excess') ≥ £500,000

Spreading provisions

Amount of excess contributions	Fractions and chargeable periods
< £500,000	No spreading required
£500,000 – £999,999	½ treated as paid in current period, ½ treated as paid in the next chargeable period
£1m – £1,999,999	$\frac{1}{3}$ treated as paid in the current period, $\frac{1}{3}$ treated as paid in each of the next 2 chargeable periods
£2m +	¼ treated as paid in the current period, ¼ treated as paid in each of the next 3 chargeable periods.

Loan relationships

A company that borrows or invests money has a loan relationship.

Trading loan relationship

- Loan for trade purposes (eg debentures issued to raise money to buy plant and machinery)
- Costs (eg interest) accruing are deductible trade expenses

Non-trading loan relationship

- Held for non-trade purposes (eg bank account held for investment purposes)
- Tax income (eg interest income) and capital profit accruing on non-trading loan relationships
- Deduct expenses and capital losses accruing from the pool of interest income.

Exam focus

Interest income is never treated as trading profit in the exam.

Intangible fixed assets ■——■ eg patents, copyrights, goodwill

Income/expenditure dealt with as trading income in accounts. No adjustment required if accounts properly prepared.

Income:

eg profit on disposal of IFA, royalty income

Expenditure:

eg royalty payable, loss on disposal of IFA, amortisation

Research and development

⬇

Tax deduction

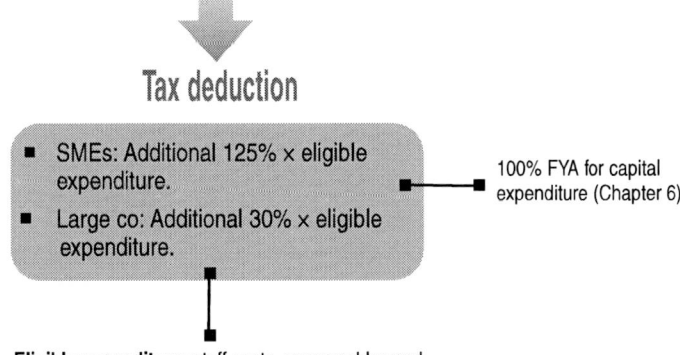

- SMEs: Additional 125% × eligible expenditure.
- Large co: Additional 30% × eligible expenditure.

100% FYA for capital expenditure (Chapter 6)

Eligible expenditure: staff costs, consumables and software

Property income – income from land and buildings

- Mainly use same rules as for an individual
- ◄◄ See Chapter 2
- Losses can, however, be set against any other income and not just other property income

Mortgage interest

- Treatment is different from an individual.
- Deductible under the loan relationship rules, *not* as a property business expense.

Furnished holiday accommodation

Furnished holiday accommodation must be

- In the UK or elsewhere in EEA
- Furnished
- Let on a commercial basis
- Available for letting for 210 days in the accounting period
- Actually let for 105 days in the 210 day period
- Not in **longer term occupation** for more than 155 days in a 12 month period

Continuous periods of more than 31 days during which the accommodation is in the same occupation

Double taxation relief

eg withholding tax

- Unilateral relief where UK and foreign taxes suffered on same income
- Maximum relief lower of:
  - UK tax on foreign income and
  - Foreign tax suffered

Offsetting deductions

eg qualifying charitable donations

Set against:

- UK income first, then
- Foreign income with lowest marginal overseas tax rate

Example

A UK company receives overseas rental income of £80,000 net of 15% withholding tax. The company's only other income in the year to 31 March 2014 is trading income of £2,000,000.

The taxable overseas income is:

£80,000 × $^{100}/_{85}$ = £94,118

The UK tax payable is:

£94,118 × 23% = £21,647 less DTR of £14,118 (as this is lower than the UK tax).

20: Additional aspects of corporation tax

Notes

21: Value added tax

This chapter looks at some more complex areas of VAT in particular the impact of partial exemption on input VAT recovery and the VAT issues relating to property transactions.

It also covers the capital goods scheme and the VAT issues of trading with other EU, and non-EU, states.

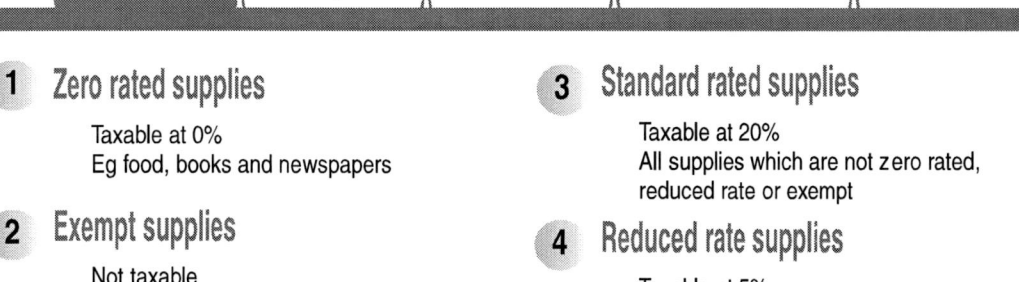

| Supplies | Partial exemption | Property transactions | Capital goods scheme | Overseas aspects |

1 Zero rated supplies

Taxable at 0%
Eg food, books and newspapers

2 Exempt supplies

Not taxable
Eg insurance, education and health services

3 Standard rated supplies

Taxable at 20%
All supplies which are not zero rated,
reduced rate or exempt

4 Reduced rate supplies

Taxable at 5%
Eg fuel for domestic use, smoking
cessation products and contraceptives

Alert! A person making only exempt supplies cannot recover VAT on inputs. Contrast this with a
person making zero rated (taxable supplies) who can recover VAT on inputs.

Supply of goods or services?

Important to differentiate as different rules may apply eg place of supply rules.

Supply of goods	Supply of services
Treated as a supply of goods:	Treated as a supply of services:
■ Supply of any form of power, heat, etc	■ Goods hired to someone
■ Taking goods out of a business for non-business use	■ Goods lent to someone for use outside the business

Multiple (or combined) supply

Split into components. The appropriate VAT rate is applied to each component.

Single (or composite) supply

Cannot be split into components. One (the main) VAT rate applies.

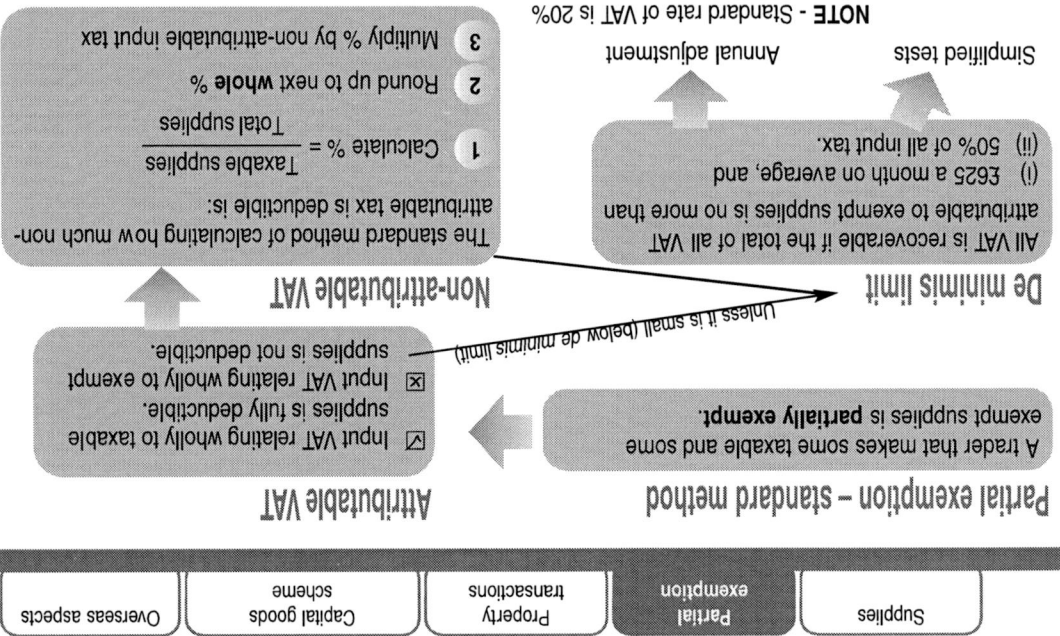

NOTE - Standard rate of VAT is 20%

Partial exemption – standard method

A trader that makes some taxable and some exempt supplies is **partially exempt.**

Attributable VAT

☑ Input VAT relating wholly to taxable supplies is fully deductible.

☒ Input VAT relating wholly to exempt supplies is not deductible.

Unless it is small (below de minimis limit)

Non-attributable VAT

The standard method of calculating how much non-attributable tax is deductible is:

1. Calculate % = $\dfrac{\text{Taxable supplies}}{\text{Total supplies}}$
2. Round up to next **whole** %
3. Multiply % by non-attributable input tax

De minimis limit

All VAT is recoverable if the total of all VAT attributable to exempt supplies is no more than

(i) £625 a month on average, and

(ii) 50% of all input tax.

Simplified tests

Annual adjustment

Simplified tests

Two simplified test are available for partial exemption

Test one

All VAT is recoverable if

- Total input tax is no more than £625 per month on average; and
- Value of exempt supplies is no more than 50% of total supplies

Test two

All VAT is recoverable if

- Total input tax less input tax directly attributable to taxable supplies is no more than £625 per month on average; and
- Value of exempt supplies is no more than 50% of total supplies

- If either test is met all input VAT for the VAT period is recoverable
- If fail both tests apply standard method to the VAT period

Annual adjustments

Apply simplified tests to VAT year.
- If meet either test all input VAT recoverable
- If fail both tests apply standard test to VAT year

Determine amount payable to/ repayable from HMRC

De minimis in one year means provisional recovery of in-year input tax in following year. Annual adjustment only.

Land and buildings

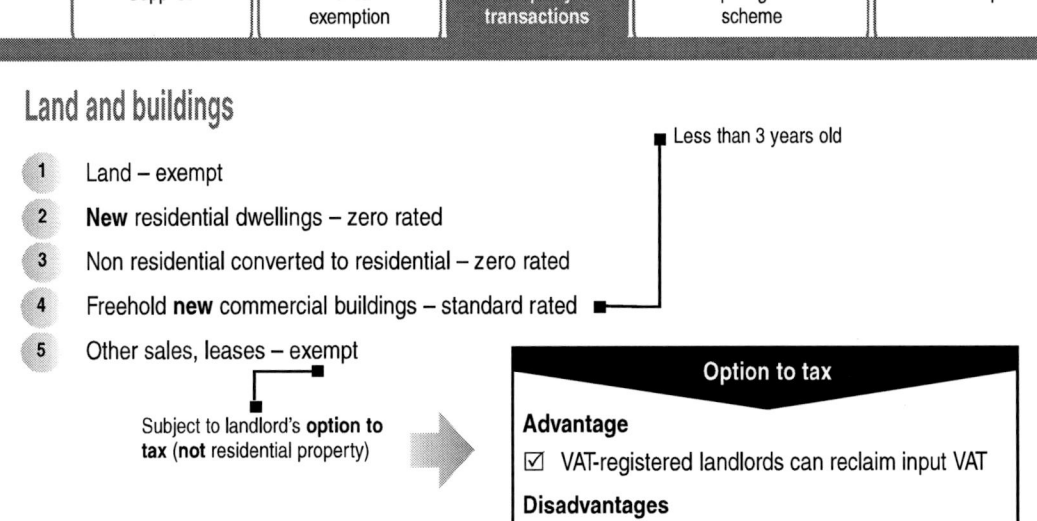

1 Land – exempt

2 **New** residential dwellings – zero rated

3 Non residential converted to residential – zero rated

4 Freehold **new** commercial buildings – standard rated ■ ── ■ Less than 3 years old

5 Other sales, leases – exempt

Subject to landlord's **option to tax** (**not** residential property)

Option to tax

Advantage

☑ VAT-registered landlords can reclaim input VAT

Disadvantages

☒ Must charge VAT on rent

☒ Expensive for non-registered tenants

Capital goods scheme

Initial recovery of input tax on **certain capital goods** is adjusted to reflect variations in the taxable use of those goods. ■

- Applies to:
  - **Land and buildings** costing £250,000 or more – adjusted over 10 years
  - **Computers** costing £50,000 or more – adjusted over 5 years
  - **Boats or aircraft** costing £50,000 or more – adjusted over 5 years

Adjustment each year:
- Difference between taxable use percentage for 1st year and taxable use percentage for current year
- × 1/10 (land) or 1/5 (computers, boats & aircraft).

On sale:
- Normal annual adjustment, PLUS
- Further adjustment for remaining years assuming taxable use of 0% (exempt sale) or 100% (taxable sale)

| Supplies | Partial exemption | Property transactions | Capital goods scheme | Overseas aspects |

Inside the EU

Dispatches
The supply is zero rated if the customer is VAT registered and his registration number is shown on the invoice. Otherwise the supply uses normal UK VAT rates.

Acquisitions
VAT (calculated using UK rates) is only due if there is a taxable acquisition (ie the acquisition of taxable goods by a taxable person). The VAT due is shown on the next VAT return by the UK buyer of the goods.

Outside the EU

Exports
Exports of goods to outside the EU are zero rated.

Imports
Imports of goods from outside the EU are subject to VAT at the same rate as on a sale within the UK, at the point of entry into the UK.

Supply of services (EU or Non-EU)

- Reverse charge system if customer is UK VAT registered trader

Takes place where:
- Supplier is, if customer not a relevant business person (B2C)
- Customer is, if customer is a relevant business person (B2B)

22: Stamp taxes

Topic List

Stamp duty

Stamp duty reserve tax

Stamp duty land tax

You must understand the scope of the different stamp taxes, be able to calculate the relevant charges and understand when an exemption may be available.

Stamp duty

Paid by transferor on transfers of shares by physical **document**.

■ Also known as an 'Instrument'

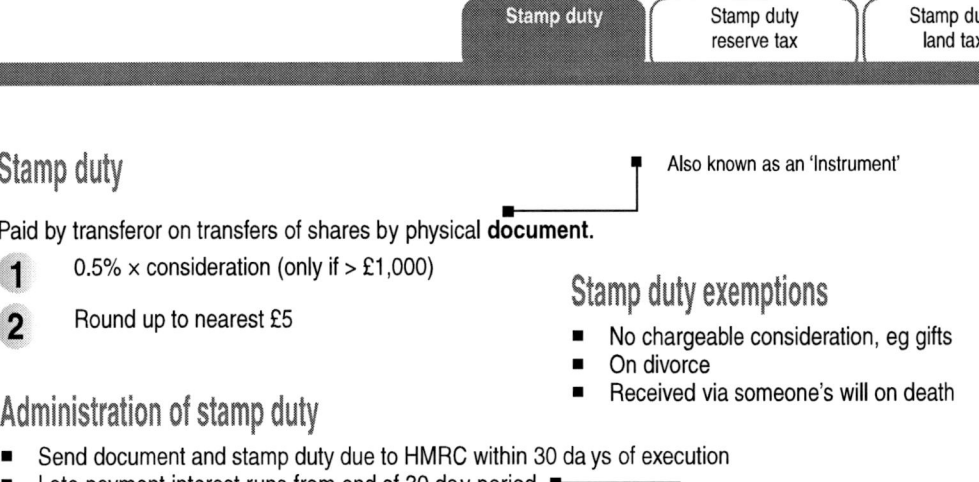

1 0.5% × consideration (only if > £1,000)

2 Round up to nearest £5

Stamp duty exemptions

■ No chargeable consideration, eg gifts
■ On divorce
■ Received via someone's will on death

Administration of stamp duty

■ Send document and stamp duty due to HMRC within 30 days of execution
■ Late payment interest runs from end of 30 day period
■ Penalty for late document:
  – ≤ 1 year late: Lower of £300 and unpaid duty
  – > 1 year late: Higher of £300 and unpaid duty

■ Round down to nearest £5
■ Only charged if > £25

Stamp duty reserve tax   ■——■ No charge if no consideration

Paid on transfers of shares not caught by stamp duty,
ie paperless transactions

1   0.5% × consideration

2   Do not round

SDRT exemptions

- No chargeable consideration, eg gifts
- On divorce
- Received via someone's will on death

Administration of SDRT

- Collected automatically via stockbrokers
- Due on:
  - 7th day of month following month of contract
  - 14 calendar days after trade date if can be made by CREST
- No penalty if paid within 60 days of contract date

22: Stamp taxes

Stamp duty land tax

Also charged on lease premium + net present value (NPV) of rent
- **Premium**: No 0% band if non-residential rent ≥£1,000 pa
- **NPV**: Max 1%

Payable by purchaser on land transactions eg
- Transfer of freehold land
- Assignment of lease
- Grant of lease

15% rate for companies purchasing residential property valued at >£2,000,000

Rate (%)	Residential	Non-residential	Disadvantaged areas Residential & non-residential
0	£125,000	£150,000	£150,000
1	£125,001 – £250,000	£150,001 – £250,000	£150,001 – £250,000
3	£250,001 – £500,000	£250,001 – £500,000	£250,001 – £500,000
4	£500,001 – £1,000,000	Over £500,000	Over £500,000
5	£1,000,001 – £2,000,000	N/A	N/A
7	Over £2,000,000	N/A	N/A

SDLT exemptions

- No chargeable consideration, eg gifts
- On divorce
- Received via someone's will on death

SDLT administration

- File land transaction return (even if no SDLT payable)
- Within 30 days of transaction
- Also pay tax within 30 days of transaction
- Late payment interest from end of 30 day period to day before SDLT paid
- Penalties for late filing:
  - Up to 3 months late: £100 automatic penalty
  - Over 3 months late: £200 automatic penalty
  - Over 1 year late: tax geared penalty up to amount of SDLT payable

23: Ethics

Topic List

The topics covered in this chapter are essential knowledge for the whole of your Taxation studies.

They ensure that your advice and communication is appropriate and in keeping with the ICAEW's requirements.

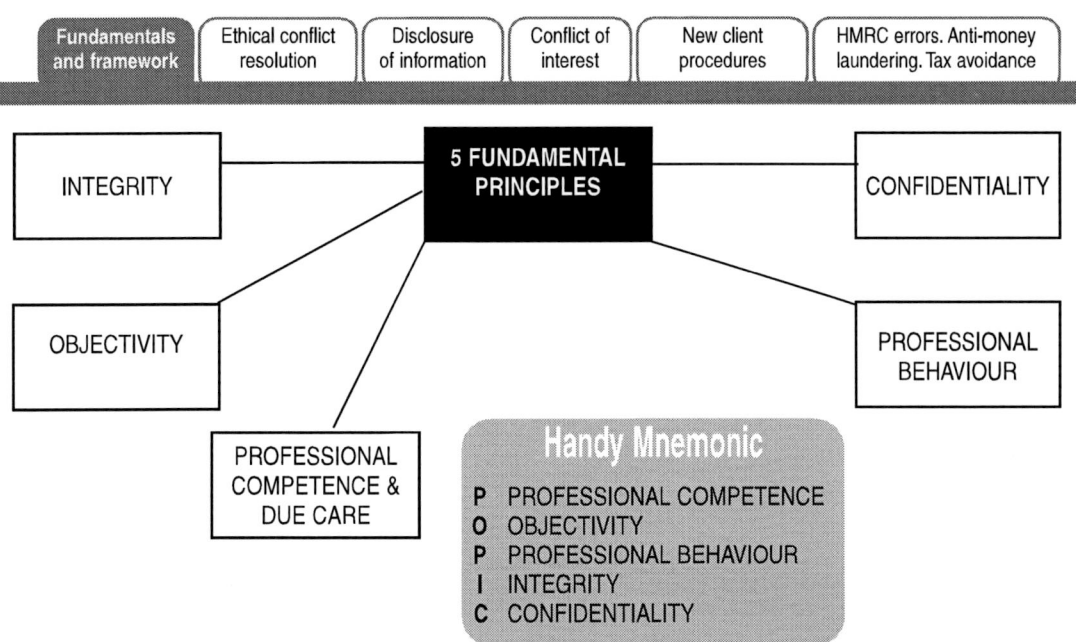

INTEGRITY

5 FUNDAMENTAL PRINCIPLES

CONFIDENTIALITY

OBJECTIVITY

PROFESSIONAL BEHAVIOUR

PROFESSIONAL COMPETENCE & DUE CARE

Handy Mnemonic

P PROFESSIONAL COMPETENCE
O OBJECTIVITY
P PROFESSIONAL BEHAVIOUR
I INTEGRITY
C CONFIDENTIALITY

1 Integrity

Being straightforward and honest in all professional and business relationships.

2

Objectivity

Obligation not to compromise professional or business judgement because of:

- Bias
- Conflict of interest, or
- Undue influence of others

3 Professional competence

- Attain and maintain professional knowledge and skill

- So clients or employers receive competent professional service

- Based on current developments in practice, legislation and techniques

- Appropriate training and supervision

- Make clear to clients any limitations relating to the service being provided to avoid misinterpretation

Due care

Act diligently in accordance with applicable technical and professional standards when providing professional services

4 Confidentiality

Obligation not to **use** or **disclose** confidential information acquired in the course of professional and business relationships, even in a social environment.

UNLESS:

PRIVATE AND CONFIDENTIAL

- You have specific and proper authorisation by the client/employer
- There is a legal or professional right to do so

5 Professional behaviour

- Comply with laws and regulations
- Protect reputation of the profession

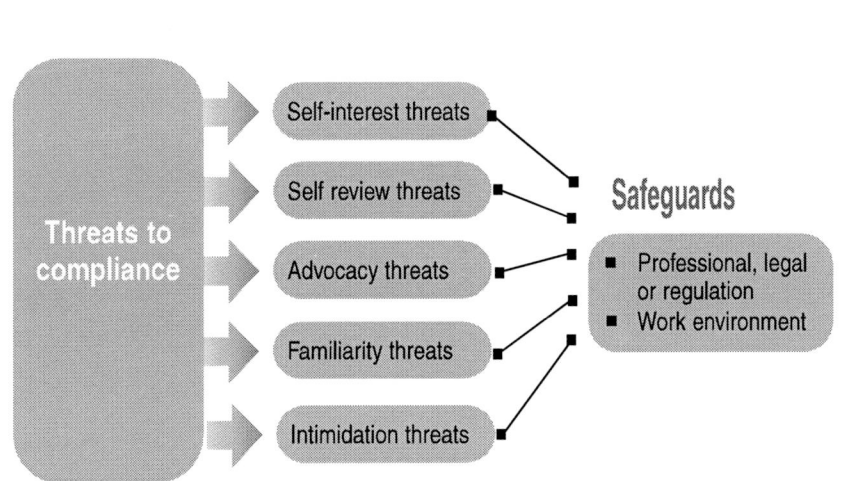

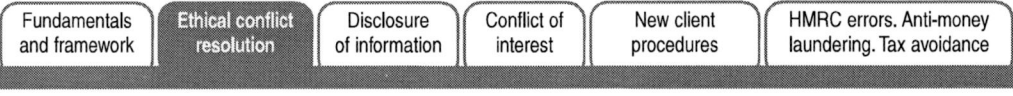

Resolving an ethical conflict ━━━■ Whether formal or informal process

Consider:
- Relevant facts
- Relevant parties
- Ethical issues involved
- Fundamental principles related to the matter in question
- Established internal procedures
- Alternative courses of action

Seek internal advice if remains unresolved ━━━■ Document issue and details

Seek legal advice if necessary ━━━■ ICAEW confidential ethics helpline

Last resort: withdraw from team or resign

Allowed to disclose confidential information:

1 When it is allowed by law and client or employer **properly authorises** it.

2 When **required by law** to do so:

- Production of documents for legal proceedings

- Disclosure to the appropriate public authorities eg under anti-money laundering legislation

3 When there is a **professional duty** or right to do so.

Consider

- Will disclosure harm any interested party's interests?

- Is all known information correct?

Should take reasonable steps to identify circumstances that could pose a conflict of interest.

Conflict situations

Where a firm acts for both:

- A husband and wife in a divorce settlement

- A company and its directors in their personal capacity

Consider:
- Separate engagement teams
- Confidentiality agreements
- Regular reviews

Alert! Do not act if one of the 5 fundamental principles is unacceptably threatened.

Safeguards

- Notify the client of the conflict of interest
- Notify all parties that acting for two or more parties in a conflict matter
- Notify the client that not acting exclusively for any one client
- Obtain consent of the relevant parties to act

Accountant as agent

- When prepares documents *on behalf of* a client

- Client retains responsibility for accuracy of documents

- Tax compliance work eg preparing and submitting a tax return

- Client must sign the return before it is submitted

- Not normally liable if information incorrect

Engagement letter

Set out if acting as principal or agent and scope of responsibilities of client and accountant

Accountant as principal

- When provides tax advice *to* the client

- Accountant takes full responsibility and may be liable to the taxpayer if advice incorrect or inappropriate

- May still accept the engagement even if does not have required skill (must seek advice)

Low risk

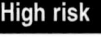

High risk

Professional indemnity insurance

Required if ICAEW qualified member in public practice.

Minimum requirement:

If gross fee income less than £600,000

- 2½ times gross fee income, min £100,000

Otherwise

- minimum £1.5 million

Cover to remain in place for at least two years after ceasing to be in public practice. It is recommended that cover to be maintained for six years.

Data protection

- Notify Information Commissioner's Office (ICO) and be entered on ICO register of data controllers
- Criminal offence to fail to do so

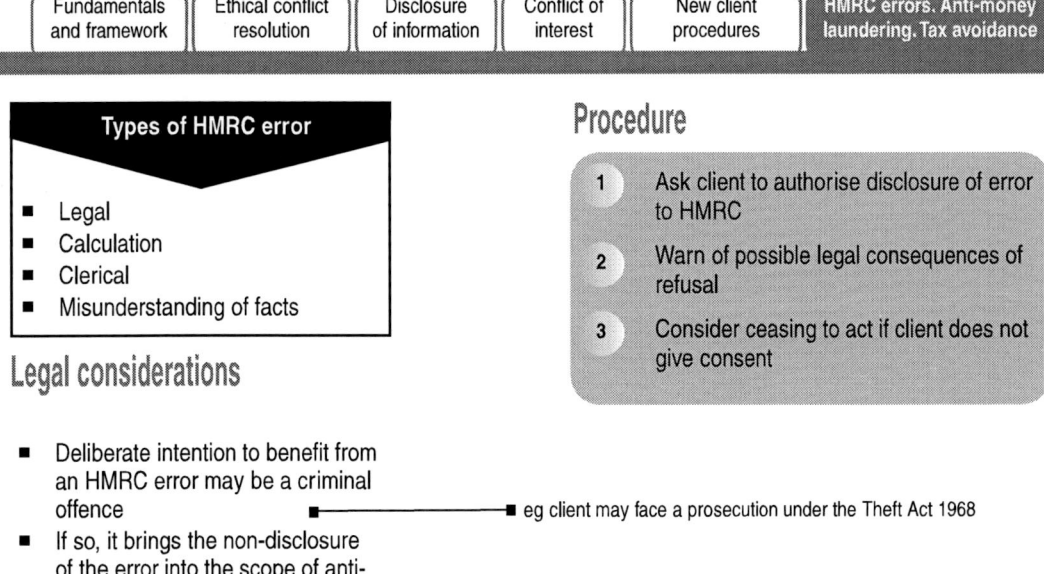

Types of HMRC error

- Legal
- Calculation
- Clerical
- Misunderstanding of facts

Legal considerations

- Deliberate intention to benefit from an HMRC error may be a criminal offence
- If so, it brings the non-disclosure of the error into the scope of anti-money laundering legislation

■ eg client may face a prosecution under the Theft Act 1968

▶▶ See below

Procedure

1. Ask client to authorise disclosure of error to HMRC

2. Warn of possible legal consequences of refusal

3. Consider ceasing to act if client does not give consent

Anti-money laundering

Money laundering is the attempt to conceal the true origin or ownership of the proceeds of criminal activity or terrorist funding ('criminal property') – including the proceeds of tax evasion, benefits obtained through bribery and benefits arising from non-compliance with regulatory requirements.

Must register with an appropriate anti-money laundering supervisory authority.

1 Client checking, record keeping and internal suspicion reporting

    → Appointment of a Money Laundering Reporting Officer (MLRO); client checking procedures

2 Not doing or discussing anything that might prejudice an investigation

    → No word or action that might 'tip off' the money launderers that they are (or may come) under investigation

3 Report suspicions (on reasonable grounds) of money laundering

    → Report to:

- The Money Laundering Reporting Officer
- Serious Organised Crime Agency (use suspicious activity report (SAR))

Watch client confidentiality

Penalties: Offences tried in Magistrates' Court or Crown Court - unlimited fines and imprisonment possible

Tax avoidance

- Lawful tax effective method of avoiding/ reducing amount of tax due.
- No intention of misleading HMRC.

Tax evasion

- Unlawful way of avoiding/ reducing amount of tax due
- Misleading HMRC eg

  1 Suppressing information

  2 Providing deliberately false information

Important case law

Ramsay Ltd v IRC, & other cases

Disregard transactions with no commercial purpose
but not always eg where purpose of legislation unclear

→ Success of aggressive tax avoidance is uncertain

HMRC can challenge abusive tax avoidance arrangements using the GAAR

Notes

Notes

Notes

Notes

Notes